...s for a L...
...luck with your ...
...Knowing you like I b...
...ll get it. Be careful & you...
...y will come soon when the big b...
...et you home

—Duane
47 Days
Short

So glad you
finally made
my flight baby
several more tim...
before you see
Fresh ... ste...
Good luck!

Judy ...
USL

...wish the
plane would
... to the right
road!

...drunk man
Paint man...
...thing

Gomer (pile) was glad to recieve
you in our squad, keep it kool and
try to do your best.
I mad
PFC Romero 180 Days

"Gomer,"
To one of the best guys
I've known in a long time.
Be good, & if you can't be
good, Be good at it! OK and
Don't out any one any slack
especially him. (know what I
mean)
A friend
Always
Frank
(don't you)
Jet
(Cherry Boy)

These are things other soldiers wrote on the front cover of Tommy's Vietnam
'Short Timer Calendar' just before Tommy got to come home.

By the Grace of
God
A Promise Kept

SHEREE (TIGER) EVANS

Paperback-Press
an imprint of A & S Publishing
A & S Holmes, Inc.

ISBN: 0692368760
ISBN-13: 978-0692368763

Tribute

This book is a loving dedication to a forgotten Vietnam Veteran. To my love, my hero, the man that taught me about life, love, laughter and gave me the best years of my life, thank you for loving me, my sweet Tommy.

CONTENTS

Acknowledgements

My heartfelt thanks go to my buddy Jim Vinson. Jim's another Vietnam Veteran who, since I started this book, gave his life to Glio from Agent Orange exposure. He is the one who titled By the Grace of God a Promise Kept, and I'll always cherish his help and support in keeping me on track to get the pages finished. Rest in Peace, my friend.

Jim Vinson

Prayer

Please, let us pray.

Lord, please bless all of our military. For those fighting in battle, I pray You give to them the love, strength, guidance, faith and support they need to carry them through such a trying and difficult time.

The decisions these soldiers have to make are demanding, but please let them not be burdened. Help them have clear thoughts, restful moments and always have faith in You Dear God. Allow that faith to work as a shield. May they feel the warm glow of Your luminous light at all times.

With their knowledge of You and Your love for Your children, give these men and women hope. May their hope, prayers and faith in You through their trying times, help bring them safely home to their family and friends.

Thank You oh gracious Lord for all You do.

Amen!

Life As We Knew It

Before Our Lives Embraced

Edward Tommy Evans was born in Norfolk, Virginia, on July 1ˢᵗ 1950. His father was a boxer in the Navy, and his mother a devoted homemaker.

Tommy's mother Mable died right before Christmas...he was only ten years old. For that little boy his mama was his first love. She was so sweet, gentle and always protecting and nurturing Tommy. She was the type of woman that glowed when she walked into a room. She had the most warming smile and God given beauty.

Christmas, for most, would be getting ready for the holidays, going through the excitement of putting up a tree, cold weather and possibly snow on the ground so snowmen could be built. However, not for Tommy, the holidays turn out to be the saddest times in this little boy's life.

His sister became his caregiver. Always looking out for him and bossing him around, lovingly leading him in the right direction. They shared a bond other siblings only dreamed about.

When their father was out to sea, the two loved their time with their aunt and uncle, but mostly Tommy loved spending time with his grandfather. He spent many a day over at his grandparents' house. His grandfather was his buddy. A man he looked up to and loved with all his heart. Grandson and grandfather simply keeping each other company, they'd go fishing and share life together.

His mom passing took its toll on Tommy, but he was absolutely devastated when one day he found his grandfather who had hung himself. The old man's suicide was almost more than the eleven year old could handle, but life went on.

Beauford, Tommy's father, was rough on his children. When the man came home from sea, he would give the '*white glove treatment*' expecting everything to be perfect. Tommy felt he had to grow up fast. His sister ultimately fell in love and got married leaving Tommy to feel alone, especially when his father was around. The teenage boy couldn't wait to join the Marines and leave Claire road.

At eighteen years old, he did just that. Everyone liked Tommy and in boot camp he inherited the nickname Gomer (after a popular television character) from his comrades because he would march in wrong formation or he might have two left boots on. He not stupid by no means, but he hadn't gotten used to the routine yet.

Tommy told me about having to wake up every morning to the sound of metal cans being thrown down onto the concrete floor. Then they were expected to make their beds up to where a coin would bounce off the covers, get dressed then stand at attention for inspection. He had a hard time doing all of this, as did the other soldiers, but Tommy vowed to overcome the situation.

One day he bewildered the officer in charge when he was standing at attention almost before the sound of the cans being thrown stopped. Tommy had manage to pull the wool over their eyes when he decided to make his bed perfectly, then he dressed and slept that night under his cot. When they came in, he was ready to stand at attention without doing much of anything to get ready.

As time would tell Gomer got orders for Vietnam. There were a lot of teenagers that joined up for different reasons, but most wanted to prove that their lives had some kind of meaning. They wanted to belong and share times with others their age.

I really don't think they knew what they were faced with, or how terrible war is. They were being trained to fight. To kill or be killed but they would do what they could to stay alive. These teens were fighting a man's war, as they still do today, facing the unthinkable!

They tolerated all that Vietnam brought; monsoons, swamps, the insects, snakes and more. These young folks carried their guns and ammo, ready to shoot to defend our country. Protect their brothers in arms. It was their special bond, because they counted on each other to stay alive. The air was still, hot and humid. Sweat poured off of them, it was a nightmare of a battleground, but most battlegrounds are. No alarm clocks, no sleeping in a safe warm bed with a pillow, not being able to take showers and wear clean clothes.

Civilians were the lucky ones; safe and sound in our homes in America. Can you imagine how hard it must have been for those boys to actually have to kill another human being? Or be killed by another young man they didn't even know but was called the enemy?

Being the smallest in his platoon, Gomer was chosen as a tunnel rat. He faced dark, narrow, short tunnels, with little air, which could possibly be booby trapped with explosives. Not to mention the enemy lurking around waiting to pounce.

If he wasn't in the tunnels, Gomer carried the dead soldiers, our soldiers, to the copters. It broke his heart, but he knew it had to be done. He was also a mortar man. Wearing so many hats, he had to be tough or die trying.

He remembered drinking warm coke they would get for a treat or ice cream that would drop from the copters. It melted as fast as it fell, but they ate it anyway. Camel cigarettes would also fall from the sky. Most of the men smoked back then, so that was something they really looked forward to.

However, the worst thing to fall to the ground was Agent Orange. They sprayed it from the airplanes, along with other chemicals to clear the jungles, so the enemy could be seen better.

What were the higher ups thinking? It was all about Power! Didn't they know what this would do to our troops? They couldn't have cared about our men getting that toxic chemical on their skin and in their eyes or it wouldn't have been sprayed so much.

Agent Orange was in everything and it was everywhere. The soldiers couldn't just go home and shower. The toxic stuff soaked into their clothing and boots from the marshes and waters they crawled or walked through. It was terrible.

The first time Tommy/Gomer was wounded he was hit in the abdomen. There was no hospital for him to go to, the enemy was everywhere. The medics in the field could only do so much! His wound stayed open for four days.

When Tommy/Gomer survived being wounded again, this time shot in the cheek, he received two purple hearts. He came home with an honorable discharge to try and resume his life.

Tommy was a teenager when he went to Vietnam but he came home a war-torn man. Upon his return, he realized his world had changed. Feeling shunned by society because people didn't greet him with a smile, or thank him for his heroic service to our country. Instead they spit on him and called him baby killer. His own nephews even asked him how many men he killed. He couldn't believe it was all happening like this. Coming home was supposed to be a happier time.

Tommy, like so many of our men, felt betrayed and isolated. He and others put their life on the line or sacrificed their life, so we in America could have our freedoms. But he loved his service buddies and was proud to see the American flag flying on his home ground. It gave him purpose and stability, making fighting the war worth it. He and most of his comrades, no matter how they were treated, would go back in a heartbeat to defend Ole Glory.

He couldn't get a job, but he did the best he could on the small amount of disability he got from the VA for getting wounded. The feeling that other Americans were unappreciative of what he and his comrades had done to help them keep their freedom, weighed heavy on his heart, but he still did his duty and worked for the Civil Service.

He decided to join a motorcycle club. He then opened a shop to work on bikes. The only problem was some didn't feel they should pay for the work he did. After all, they were buds.

Unable to handle it anymore, he felt it was best to close up and leave town. He ended up in Lubbock, Texas.

He found work as a maintenance man for the city. He also worked part time at the KOA campground, cutting grass, and doing maintenance in exchange for a place to live, which was an old school bus that had been transformed into an RV. He loved it.

However, his medical problems followed him. He had loss of hearing, PTSD and his feet were constantly raw and aching. He was told this was jungle rot, but it wouldn't clear up no matter what the doctors tried.

This was only the beginning.

Below are Tommy's own words about Nam.

①

I was asked how I felt when
I came back from Viet Nam.
I guess I was in shock just like
I was when I landed in Danang
early in the morning, I couldn't believe
that on one side of the world I was
killing kids the other side was protesting
I was with A/7 1st MAR DIV.
DANANG
BEN WA
TRAN TREE
~~the~~ e OkLAhomA City
I was a tunnel RAt, I did MINE sweeps
Set out ~~Live~~ LANE mines Stood
guard got shot twice once in the
JAr once in the Belly when I
got Back my Nephews were SMALL
but they knew About the wAr. They
Asked me the 1st morning home how
mANy people did I kill my Brother
LAw ~~wAs A drAft Taggor~~ he went
to college to this day he makes
Fun of me because I sent tApes
home Letters home sAying the
truth I wAs scAred ANd Lived
one dAy AT A time

I was 18 yrs old. I just left
home because my mom died of
cancer when I was 10 the night
before christmas. My grandfather
touching himself the night before
christmas of the next yr. My sister
married at 17 I stayed and went to
school cleaned house. I was ready
to leave home. My dad said I would
never make it I wanted to prove
something to him. When I got back
to the world I was very confused I
couldn't get a job. I was told VA
would help you. well they didn't I
got 23.00 a moth for being shot twice
and bad feet no help in getting
a job my hearing was bad but they
said it would get butter it never did.
Now the VA wants to help but it
still missed up people say why did
you wait 20 yrs. The system has been
so screwed up only the people
who have been in the system
understand jungle rot was cold
4 different things when you went
to VA the doctors didn't know

③

what they were looking At much
less how to treat it EA, time
you went you got different doctors
with different iteas, Flash Backs
No one knew how to treat it. And
if you went to VA while working
A New job you Lost your job.
They were running people through VA
Like CAttle they hurry up And be
done with it they had A EArly out
program back then but they had not
thought About jobs For these people
or how to help them or About th VA
Benefits you didn't ever know what
you were Enetitled To. d was ready
To go back in 6 mos After d was out.
you Felt Like you were Important
your rank meant something you were
treated by how you perFormed Now
ToDAy everything we live died For
Fought For WAS Lost burn the Flag
its your right, to Express your selF iF you
were in the Service in 1965 And Burnt
the Flag you would do Life, over the yrs

④

One year we are saving the world the next yr. we are taking the money back away from programs that it took 10 yrs to get started the united states keeps falling Back one step forward one step Backwards we the people have made the difference not the gov. Our POW's have been left to die and Be Forgotton But our space program has went forward every yr. Congrass has received raises and live in 3 and 4 houses can't decide on anything we the people make life and death decisions every day that effects our life for the future. The people have Been cheated, lied to, and disgraced by our gov. to long and the people are tied oz hen(ing tightenup. work longer hours while our gov. spends money like crasy and lives likes Kings. Now our gov says familys don't spend enought time at home with our

finger up their butt saying we
just don't see how we can do
anything tell next yr, Taxes seems
likes that saves the world, Veterans
Are under more stress than ever, flash
Backs, problems, family, and its not getting
any better, when I joined the marines
if you went to Canada you went to jail
Now those same people live besides us
~~en~~ enjoy the benefits And talk About
American the beautyful, salute the flag
And ~~talke~~ talk about the united states
how sorry it is, or how great it is.
But still he lives here with the
same rights you have. I Tell All
the veterans have been done wrong And
~~cheated~~ cheated out of A great deal Now
veterans Are trying to get benefits they
should have received 20 yrs ago.
And still every one says why didn't
you file this form 18 yrs Ago, there
wasn't A form like this 20 yrs ago.
And if there had of been No one
knew how to process it

My World

Growing Up

I was born in Santa Anna, California. My dad was in the Marines, my mom was a housewife, who tended to have mood swings, and I had four siblings.

We moved around a lot because of my dad being in the service. I remember living in Kansas City where my aunt and uncle lived across the street but further down. Then later, when my dad was discharged, we moved to Springfield, Missouri and I finished growing up there on Normal Street.

How ironic, I didn't feel there was anything normal about my life, growing up and going through a lot of wrongful time due to my mother's medical problems. One of my older brothers, who could do no wrong in my mom's eyes, was mean to me. You just don't forget when you're mistreated, not even when you get older. My mother allowed him to treat me badly and she threatened to kill me if I told my dad because most of the time Dad was at work. He didn't have a clue of what was happening.

My father was the best dad ever! When he asked my siblings to go with him to visit his family they said no. When he asked me, I said yes and then it was from then on I would go with him whenever I could. I felt safe and loved by my father. Like I said, he didn't know what was going on while he was working nor was I going to tell being so young I was afraid he wouldn't believe me, but of all I was afraid my mom would kill me like she said.

As I grew up and life at home didn't get any better. One by one my brothers and sisters left home most of them joined the service. I went to a private Catholic school and there I felt stable and safe. I loved riding my bike over to my, my maternal grandparents' house.

Grandma would fix something to eat and I would stay with them all day. Grandma and I would put together jigsaw puzzles. Those are some of my fondest memories along with taking naps in her bedroom where the walls were soft green. That color has stayed in my mind, and I painted my bedroom with it—

soothing and calm. They were the sweetest, most loving grandparents and so down to earth. They didn't have a car so my mom took grandma to the store and her doctor's appointment. Mom actually treated her parent's decently.

At the age of sixteen, I realized I could work so I found employment at a restaurant in downtown Springfield. I met a nice guy that I really liked. He had long hair and rode a motorcycle, but he was so nice to me. I introduced him to my family and my mother instantly didn't like him and was against me seeing him.

Mom went behind my back arranged for me to go out with her friend's grandson Mark, who was coming home on leave. I told her I didn't want to go because I liked the boyfriend I had. She took me into the bedroom and whipped me trying to force me to say I would go out with him. I didn't give in until I had black and blue marks on my legs and a deep hurt in my heart that she might really kill me.

Months went by and before I knew it and I liked Mark okay so when he asked me to marry him, I figured it was a good way to get out of the house. Stupid I know, but I was so young and naïve it sounded like a good thing. I was getting married to Mom's friend's grandson and she was pleased.

My mom and Mark's grandma planned my whole wedding, cutting my hair, and wedding dress handmade. As much as I wanted to finish high school, and didn't want to leave my dad, I went through with it on the promised that if I married him I could finish school overseas. That was kind of exciting, but the promise was empty and the beginning of many lies and wrong doings.

During the time my husband was in the military, I put up with a lot of abuse, but he had a good carrier so I put up with it. Then one day he told me he was going to get out of the service and go into business with his dad and that we were going to move to Austin, TX.

I really didn't want to do that, but he was my husband so I had to go along. It was a bad time in life. Mark wouldn't work half the time, while I was working myself to death just trying to make ends meet. He abused me all the time, but when he put a gun to my head, it was the last straw. That marriage lasted for six years before I wised up and divorced him.

This was a very depressed time in my life. After the divorce started going out to night clubs. One night in particular I took some pills and had some drinks. I didn't want to live any longer. Today I realize that wasn't me; it was devil working on me, calling me, trying to get me to enter hell's gate.

Thank God for His help because that night encountered a guardian angel on earth. I do believe God works through certain angelic beings to help those in need.

After I mixed the pills and alcohol, I started to really get messed up. I don't remember what happened after that, but I kind of remember someone putting me in the shower and turning the cold water on me. I felt wet, but that's all I remember about that, too.

I have no idea who my guardian angel was. It could have been a man or a woman, either way, they took me home, put me in the shower, then dress me in my pajamas and put me in my own bed. I was safe.

I woke up the next day in my apartment felling like hell, praising the Lord for my guardian angel and truly glad it was my day off. I started to cry and asked God, why? *"Why? Doesn't anyone love me? I work, I pay my share and I try to be a good person. Is it so much to ask to find the right one to love me? Love me for who I am; someone that won't try to control me or change me?"*

Then I met someone. I thought he might be the one. He was so nice to me. Charismatic and older, I felt at ease. One night I let him stay at my house. Big, big mistake.

I had worked my waitress shift and was glad to be off and on my way home. However when I got there and opened the door, my heart fell to my feet. My apartment was empty. Not only was *he* gone, but so was all my furniture, television console everything. The whole apartment was empty. I was in shock?

Everything I'd worked for all those years….gone. Nothing to show for my life my hard work. Heartbreak was all I had now. I sat on the floor and cried myself to sleep.

The next day I woke up to a knock on the door. It was him and he had a gun pointing at me and smelled of whiskey.

BY THE GRACE OF GOD, A PROMISE KEPT

"Come on, let's go." He said.

I was so afraid I didn't argue. "Where did you get this car?" I asked.

"I sold the stuff from the apartment. I'm taking you back to Lubbock."

My mind was in a whirl. "Lubbock? Why?" I asked questions but he ignored me then he hit me in the face and told me to shut up. I knew the gun was by his side, and he continued to drink, so I didn't try my luck. Life was unfair, but I'd already had one bout with the devil and I didn't want to have another one.

Once we got Lubbock he slowed down at a stop sign. It was slower than he'd had the car since we left Austin. That's when I felt it was my chance to jump out and run for my life. I did.

I ran toward a couple that was out in their yard. I screamed "He's got a gun, help me, please."

They were so nice and rushed me into their house. I immediately called the police, but apparently they didn't find him. However, I never saw him again. Thank God.

At least I was in a place where I knew people; I didn't have anything but the clothes on my back and my purse. Thankfully I kept my money in my purse at all times. I didn't have a bank account in Austin. Hell, I didn't have anything in Austin. That made my decision to stay in Lubbock.

I called a friend and she let me stay with her. I got my old job back at the Western Sizzling, and soon got into a routine. Life was getting better.

I went out dancing one night and met a guy. He seemed to be pretty nice, but once again I found myself at the hands of an abuser. It seemed like I couldn't attract anyone but this kind of person. What was wrong with me?

This guy beat me up bad, kicked me and broke my nose. Thank God...once again...for the girls I worked with. They saved me. I had learned my lesson

Two friends, one an older waitresses I worked with, the other a younger man who cooked where I worked, said they had a nice guy for me to meet. No more men! I was done. Or so I thought.

It took me a few days to say yes. I was afraid to trust another guy; however, I didn't want to be alone for the rest of my life either. Really all I wanted was to be loved. Why couldn't anyone love me? My eyes were black, my face bruised from my attacker, but yet my friends reassured me this man was a sweetheart.

I knew there were nice men out there...somewhere, but could I actually trust again? I prayed to God and asked Him what I should do. I don't know why, but after that prayer I felt hope. In my heart I sensed God gave me direction; I agreed to meet this friend of theirs.

My Knight in shining Armor

Our Blind Date

It was March 1st, 1986 after so much hesitation, I was going to go out on the blind date with the guy my friends knew as Speedy. I was staying with a friend from work, healing from a broken nose.

I didn't have any medical insurance so I went through a lot of pain. My nose was bandaged and my face was black and blue from the trauma. I was very self-conscience, but decided to go anyway.

It was a Saturday night in Lubbock, Texas and I was getting ready for my big date. Full of emotions, I was like a girl on her first date. Anxious, excited, nervous and apprehensive all rolled up, but I finished dressing up and fixed my hair applied makeup over my bruised face and finished with adding jewelry. Then I heard the doorbell ring. And my friend answered the door.

There he was standing outside the door, friendly smile and sparkling eyes, I could tell he was nervous as well! But he was a gentleman opening my door and talking and the more he talked the more I felt happy to know that he was the kind of man that made you feel like laughing and relaxed, and able to have a conversation with him like you known him for years.

He took me out to an Italian restaurant, that's when I found out his real name was Tommy, and we both had spaghetti. But I wanted to pay my way being our first meeting each other and I didn't want him to think I was that type of gal that wanted a man to lavish her with money because I worked most my life and I knew how hard money was come by.

We later started talking about his work his old green truck, he picked me up in he said that was a test to see my reactions to him driving up to pick me up if I would make fun of it. But I told him that I couldn't care less as long as it was running and able to provide transportation to get us where we needed to go.

I think Speedy felt embarrassed. But I didn't even have a car and I didn't even know how to drive, I was 28 and no license. Speedy/Tommy took me out dancing and that was so much fun. From that night on we became inseparable.

I had another friend closer to work so I stayed with her and he would drop me off after our dates. I was a waitress and he was maintenance man. We both had lived hard lives before our meeting, but now whatever we went through challenges. We both feel God had a hand in our intervention.

We were two lonely hearts now we were together Speedy lived and worked part time at the campground and he had this old school bus converted into a motor home complete with everything you needed to survive. The jerk I lived with for 4 wasted years of my life contacted me at work and wanted his bicycle back.

I told Speedy what nerve after I gave him all the money I made to pay my way and part went into a new vehicle that jerk was driving. But Tommy didn't want that bike so he met up with the jerk to give him the bike. I was somewhat nervous because he didn't want me going with him. Later Tommy told me he took a knife with him and he really wanted to punch his lights out but he was nice and then we were together and all was good!

We celebrated our first pizza together! No, really, we did. He took a ride on his motorcycle and that was living I felt free the wind blowing my hair and Speedy had shoulder length hair and a beard complete with mustache and I always liked that in a man made me feel like a rebel.

Tommy was thirty-six years old, eight years older than me, never married. He had bad relationships, and lived alone. We celebrated our first Easter. We made each other Easter baskets and we did that for all our holidays.

My belongings were stored at the campground, because they had rental units there and I just happened to have one with my personal stuff. Tommy asked me to live with him but I remembered one of our first dates. He asked me to go with him on a run. I said yeas, anything to be with him. He said dress casual because it being nothing fancy.

So he came by and picked me up and he had his old green rusted truck and picked me up, then we went to the campground to pick up the trailer and then we went off. Seem like a ways to go, then he pulled up and I saw a lot of birds and the odor was a bit much but I didn't complain. I had never been to a city dump and I told Tommy thank you for thinking of me, to let me have the experience of something new and was part of his job.

He couldn't help laughing and smiling and he told me later that that was another test to see if I wouldn't complain. I think I shocked him because I was totally the opposite. Then he told me that then he knew for sure I was the woman for him that he wanted to spend his life with.

I loved the way he hugged me and he kissed me all the time. And at night when I lay next to him he had his warm arms wrapped around me and I felt so safe and contented calm and peaceful. I knew Tommy wouldn't let anything happen to me.

We lived together for six months, I bought him some pots and pans because he liked to cook spaghetti and I found out what any unselfish man he was when one day I bought him a pair of boots because the ones he was wearing had a big hole in the bottom. Well he told me to take them back to the store. I had spent too much on them.

I think that was our first argument, but it wasn't a bad one. We later both agreed that I would take them back, he would get a cheaper pair, and that I would buy myself an outfit with the rest. He was happy and I felt like he was so thoughtful to not take advantage of me, that I guess that was a test I did on him to see what kind of man he was.

We both continued to work and soon bought our first mobile home and lived on the campground until one day Tommy asked me to be his wife, and I started crying, and hugged him and kissed him, then he was crying. We knew he got the answer that he wanted. How could I not say Yes! We had been on the motorcycle that day, on top of a hill, where his favorite place to ride some canyon, and I yelled from the top of the mountain, "Yes, Speedy, I will marry you!"

The Surprise Bridal Shower

A Happy Time

Ellen from the campground called me up and invited me to go out to dinner with her. We decided on my day off. Ellen had mentioned that she wanted to talk about our wedding plans. That's all it took because I was so happy to be marring Speedy and he worked there And his nickname, Speedy, was given to him because he walked so fast and worked so hard, got jobs done without wasting time., and all was good.

So it was my day off and Ellen drove by to pick me up. We lived at the campground and she asked me if I was hungry, but we had to stop by her place because she had forgotten something. I didn't think much about it and so she got out and she told me you might as well come in. It may take a few minutes. I said okay, and I got out and followed her into her home. As I reached the dinning rea a whole bunch of my friends yelled "Surprise!"

I know I was as red as a tomato. Ellen proceeded to pin a corsage on me. She thought of everything; the table and the beautiful cake with wishing well and carriage carrying the bride and groom. There was a counter full of food and snacks, and the thing that caught my eye was the chair with an umbrella hovered over the top. It was decorated so pretty. Ellen was Italian so it was a custom of theirs and that was my throne so to speak.

But it wasn't no ordinary shower, it was a lingerie shower and I glanced over at the wall, and there was this cartoon looking man figure—And one of my friends said, that's a game we will play. She said, pin the privates on the man, blindfolded. Now I really was embarrassed. I just remembered when it was my turn, I pinned it up on his ear. We all laughed and had such a good time. I realized then that God gave me the gift of friendship and I didn't know so many liked me.

There were so many beautiful gifts, all covering the tables and they told me to sit on my throne. You are Queen for the day! Then they started handing me the presents, one by one.

Silky, shear, lacy, feathers, high heels, and creams and ointments, I never seen before. I received so many naughty outfits and all you could hear was a bunch of giggles and comments, but I thought how generous they all were to me. I couldn't thank them enough for everything.

We had our refreshments and then Speedy came over, after he got off from working for the city. They had him sit in chair for a king and they gave him gifts. I am glad he got to share with our special day! That was truly a happy and memorable time, not because of all the gifts, but because how thoughtful everyone was to plan, to be there, to share, to care.

Our Wedding Plans

& Rehearsal

We told all our friends and even people we didn't even know. I had a large collection of customers as friends since I worked there all together for thirteen years. Tommy told all his friends at the city, and other people that knew him.

We decided on a date, September 12th, 1986. We tried to get all our friends involved with our celebration. They all wanted to be a part of us, because they knew we loved each other, and laughed a lot. Our faces, our smiles, we were so compatible.

However, I knew our big day wouldn't be complete without Tommy's sister from Florida being there. He wanted her there too, but didn't want her to have to spend the money to get to Lubbock.

He had no idea I was communicating with her behind his back. Brenda wouldn't have missed this special day for anything and she insisted on coming. She wouldn't have it any other way. Once I had her flight information I had to make up a reason for us to go to the airport. This was going to be such a surprise for the man I loved. My heart soared with happiness. I was in love with life.

We had our rehearsal and dinner the evening before wedding. Tommy cooked up a big pot of spaghetti. We ate then at dusk we went outside to the front lawn to do the walk through for the next day. I couldn't believe I was less than twenty four hours away from being married to the love of my life.

Rehearsal went off without a hitch, I only hoped our next task would as well. I told Tommy we had to go to the airport to pick up my aunt and uncle. I had made up two posters that said Evans Wedding Party, welcome to Lubbock. He didn't seem to mind, but that's kind of the way he was, always going with the flow. So, not just me and Tommy, but we loaded all up in several vehicles, and we arrived at airport in time to see plane arrive.

The funny thing about the whole surprise for Tommy was, he never once asked me what my aunt and uncle looked like. Then, while he was looking for some older couple, he almost walked right past his sister and her husband. That was so funny!

Once he saw her, and it registered who she was, his mouth fell wide open, and he picked her up and twirled her around. He was so happy and so was she.

One of the first things she did was give Tommy a haircut, since that was her business for many years, and made him look even more handsome. That completed the wedding rehearsal and setting up for the wedding.

Our Wedding Day—September 12th, 1986

Going to the Chapel

We all woke up the next morning. This was our big day! The one we planned on, saved up for, every payday, putting money aside for our cake, decorations, rental items. I asked Ellen's husband if he would like to give me away because my father had died back home in Missouri, the previous year.

I was sad, thinking how wonderful Speedy and my dad would have liked each other. Both Marine Veterans, and both served with honor for our country, knew what war was, and both disabled from war. My father back then, war wasn't talked about, Korea—WWII, but my father was in Marines for over 15 years. I missed my dad so much! I was his little girl—the youngest of five, but I have all the precious memories stored in my Heart, and I am so Blessed by God to have known be part of him, and know that in Heaven, he was watching over me.

We all had our breakfast, and Brenda, Tommy's sister, had family keepsakes she brought to give Tommy. Some things he made as a child, heirlooms and more. This was Tommy's first marriage, and I was so honored he chose me.

We thanked God, that morning for beautiful clear blue skies, because our wedding was taking place outside in front lawn of our mobile home. We had our breakfast, and then we knew time was getting away from us, and we had so much to do. Tommy got over 150 chairs from the city. Our friends showed up to help us set everything up. We rented a trellis, and green carpet, and podium for our old fashion country wedding.

One of Tommy's best friends, Johnny Travis, was country singer and a Vietnam brother. He came to our wedding and brought his sister and her husband. He had a record out at the time called American Citizen. We were honored when he gave us a copy of the recording, then presented us with a special printed copy of the lyrics. See below.

Johnny Travis record jacket

Johnny and Sheree

16

American Citizen

I'm an American Citizen, From the heart of this land I was born,
With a love for peace and freedom, That the powers of earth can't scorn.
I've answered the call of my brothers, To come forth and take up arms,
To protect from foreign aggression, Our cities, towns, and farms.

At first, we fought for freedom of religion, Free press, and freedom of speech,
The results of this war did travel, As far as the word could reach.
We fought again in 1812, Though reluctant to enter the fray,
Our destiny forged by the white heat of war, And Great Britain's still our ally today.

We rested from war, and were thankful, For a victory so hard won,
Little did any of us guess, then, That the worst was yet to come.
The next time we shouldered our weapons, We were shooting at father and son,
This was a sign the Blue/Gray war, Had definitely begun.

We crawled through this war for four long years, With our wives and sweethearts alone,
Awaiting the word that their menfolk, Would soon be coming home.
We rebuilt our war-torn nation, From the ground up, and spared no pain,
With a vow that the woes of warfare, Would not reach our shores again.

We entered the Spanish/American War, Quite against our will,
But it happened, no less, and who can forget, Teddy's charge at San Juan Hill?
We defeated the Germans in Europe, For a price that was so hard to pay,
And the tomb of the Unknown Soldier, Still speaks of our bravery today.

When the Japanese bombed Pearl Harbor, We were as unprepared as we could be,
But we recoiled with united effort, And drove them into the sea.
Korea, they called "Police Action," But men fought, and died all the way,
And the pain, and sorrow, and suffering, Is still burned in our hearts today.

I've since been called again to war, And although it broke my heart,
I went to that far off jungle land, And I did my little part.
I didn't want to leave my sweetheart, Or leave my dad and mom,
But I would not let my brothers go, Alone to Viet Nam.

Yes, I'm an American Citizen, Her own son tried and true,
And I'm not ashamed of the lump in my throat, When I salute the Red, White, and Blue.
So, here's to you Dear Old Uncle, May your banner ever wave,
And with God in your heart, May you always be The Land of the Free and
                                                          The Brave.

Paul, Ellen, Pat and Carl, the other owners, supplied the refreshments, and friends brought food, and there was this big building we used for our wedding reception. Tommy's friend was a DJ and bartender so he took that role at the reception.

My girlfriend, the one that introduced me and Tommy, made all the reception flowers, plants. She helped to decorate, too. My colors were pink, white and blue. It was all so beautiful decorated with balloons, streamers, bells, plants and more. The tables all had tablecloths matching my colors.

When the cake was delivered, the grocery store had sent a couple workers to help, but Tommy went over to make sure everything was right. The cake topper was so cute. It was a couple on a motorcycle. I had even made a mustache, beard and sunglasses for the little guy. Our picture sat in a frame behind the couple it to make the topper complete.

I still have the topper. Man, that was so many years ago.

We picked out our favorite songs to walk down the aisle and back once we were married. I knew when I heard 'Goin' to the Chapel' it was time for me to join the love of my life at the altar.

He took my hand and we faced each other. I even wrote something I wanted to say to Speedy at our wedding so when it came time for me to say my vows, I read it out loud. He was so surprised he started to cry, and I smiled real big and told him I loved him. God was shining on us that day!

After our vows were said and the minister pronounced us man and wife the song 'She and I' began to play. We turned toward the crowd of almost 200 and walked back down the aisle as Mr. and Mrs. Edward T. Evans. I can't explain the happiness I felt. That day could have lasted forever.

Our Babies/Cocker Spaniels

Their Unconditional Love to get Us Through

I remember when we got our first dog, Barney—we were living in Texas—it was Mother's day and I had to be at work soon and there were a bunch of Cocker Spaniel puppies. Barney waited to the last, then came out and ran over to my shoe laces and started tugging on them.

I picked him up and said, "This is the one for me."

Then he couldn't be alone so soon we drove to another small town in Texas and there we found Thelma with the prettiest white coat and the longest lashes. Her eyes were so beautiful and bright—so sweet!

Tommy and I always had the love of Barney and Thelma, our Cocker Spaniels.

Thelma and Barney

They were the love our lives—until Thelma's passing, they were always there, greeting us, comforting us, unconditionally. Then it was only Barney.

Barney kept Tommy company when I was at work. He and my husband had a special bond.

A couple of years after Thelma went to the Rainbow Bridge, Barney got really sick. We had taken him to the Humane Society, which served as a Veterinarians office, too. They were going to check him out and give us a call.

The call came in when I was at work. When I got off, Tommy came to pick me up. We then drove to get Barney. His breathing was labored when we pulled up in our drive way. I was holding him in the back seat pleased he had stayed alive to see us one last time. When Tommy stopped the car, Barney died in my arms.

Tommy and I both started crying. My husband then opened my car door, took Barney, wrapped him in his favorite blankey, then dug a hole in the backyard. That's where we buried our beloved dog with his toys.

I could see how much Tommy was crying. The two had such a bond, so Tommy stayed outside to be close to Barney, and say his farewells.

We told each other it was too hard to even think about another dog. But Tommy's sister talked him into, the following Valentines, a black and white springer spaniel. She was so cute! His sister had her in a pink collar, bed blankets, and toys—polished nails—I was working, and when I got off there my new baby was.

A name for her—Pebbles was cute, off the Flintstones—but Tommy couldn't remember the name so we decided on Patches because she was black and white. Then we knew she shouldn't be by herself so, on Tommy's birthday, Tommy and I drove across town and out of a lot of puppies decided on the one that had a black spot on his buff beige coat.

We named him Gomer after Tommy nickname in the service. We celebrated all the holidays together and enjoyed being a family.

Injured on the job

Leaving Texas Moving to Missouri

Tommy worked so hard at both his jobs. He just wouldn't stop, and one day, while at work for the City of Lubbock, he lifted something. His back popped and he was in excruciating pain.

He immediately had to go have x-rays of his back and numerous tests. He was diagnosed with two ruptured disk and they wanted to do surgery.

The city made him fill out workman's comp forms. It took a while to get the benefits, but finally some money started to come in. Before that, Tommy he couldn't work, but he also couldn't have surgery because workman's comp hadn't approved a surgeon. We were living on my income alone and his small amount of disability.

Finally, there was a surgeon workman's comp approved of. They put him in the hospital, did the surgery then fit him in heavy duty body brace. He was in the hospital for a week then had to wear the brace home. He kept it on during the day, but not at night. However, once the doctor took it off for good, the pain continued. We thought over time it would get better, but it didn't.

The doctor said he would have to do surgery again, but by this time the workman's comp money had stopped and we were once again living on only my income and his minor amount disability. We didn't know what we were going to do. Then God stepped in one more time and we were invited to go to live with my aunt in Missouri.

We sold everything we had, packed up and left Texas, but we knew Tommy would have to return for his second surgery. The VA raised his disability a little which allowed us to give my aunt a little money for permitting us to live there in her home. Tommy, nor I, would have it any other way. I wasn't working yet, but we felt obligated to help her for helping us.

Still having some of the money in savings from selling our belongings, once his surgery appointment was scheduled, we made arrangements to fly back to Lubbock. Tommy's doctor made sure he got a private room so I could have a cot and could stay with my husband.

The surgery went well. He was in the hospital about five days. This time they didn't have to put the brace on. We flew back to Springfield, MO to stay with my aunt a while longer.

I started working and Tommy filed for full disability for his back. There wasn't much he could do anymore as far as hard labor went.

Soon we found a house, and moved from my aunt's. After a while he got his full benefits, but since he couldn't really work, he took care of things at the house and I was the bread winner. We were happy, in love, and perfectly satisfied with our life that way.

All was well, or so we thought.

Hope Lodge of Oz

Cancer Strikes

Throughout the seven years we'd been married, he tried to get help for his medical problems. The VA kept put him off time after time.

When he went to a VA doctor visit for pain in his growing, they told him he had a kidney infection and gave him meds for the illness. Two weeks later a nurse called and told him not to take the pills any longer. The reason was because they could cause liver damage.

The medicine hadn't helped anyway, so we made the decision to go to a civilian doctor for a second opinion. Their results were something totally different.

We were not only told that Tommy had testicular cancer, but the pills the VA had prescribed had already done damage to his liver.

The word cancer made us both sick to our stomachs. We were so upset with the VA their wrong diagnosis. Tommy decided we should go back to the Mt. Vernon VA and talk to the doctor to tell him what the civilian physicians found.

Once we did that, the VA wanted to run more tests. For sure, without any doubt, it was testicular cancer.

They told Tommy he would have to go to Fayetteville, Arkansas for surgery. It was something neither one of us looked forward to, but it had to be done, so I went with my husband. We were lucky we had friends in Fayetteville we could stay with.

When we met Tommy's doctor, he was oriental. One of the first things Tommy asked the man was if this could have been caused by Agent Orange.

I listened to the doctor take a deep breath then let it out. He finally answered by saying yes, but he refused to put it in the records, he only told us verbally, so we couldn't prove he'd said it at all.

The surgery was around Valentine's Day in 1994. After he mended from the surgery they wanted to send him to Louisiana, to take radiation treatments, but if they did that, I wouldn't have been able to go. There wasn't even a guarantee that he would have a place to stay and we couldn't afford a motel for three months.

Tommy's sister lived in Jacksonville Florida. She wanted us to move there because only an hour away, in Gainesville, was a VA hospital where Tommy could get his treatments. However, he ended up at Shands Hospital for his treatments. We made arrangements with them, but his treatments wouldn't start for a while, so in the meantime we decided, for the second time in our marriage, we'd sell everything and move. This time to Florida.

Sheree and Tommy in Biloxi on the way to Florida

I called what Tommy was going through the 'tornado'. It seemed everything was twirling in our lives and one thing after another hit us like debris. We were wondering if it would ever go back into the clouds and leave us in peace.

Tommy felt bad, but worse of all he felt guilty for us having to move again. The tornado got darker and I reassured him everything was okay. He couldn't blame himself. If there was anyone or anything to blame, it was Agent Orange and those ordered it to be sprayed. However, I knew God had other plans.

Then our prayers were answered again. Fortunately, Tommy's brother-in-law worked at Winn-Dixie and he was able to get Tommy a room at the American Cancer Society Winn-Dixie Hope Lodge in Gainsville, Florida. It was very close to the VA Hospital and I got to stay with my husband while he was there. We took a tour of the Lodge with Tommy's sister Brenda and her husband JD. Once we moved in, I really got to know the lady in charge. Her name was Judy and we became great friends. She reminded me of the Wizard of Oz. So knowledgeable, and kind and truly wanting to help everyone. I came to call the American Cancer Society Winn-Dixie Hope Lodge our 'Hope Lodge of Oz'.

Hope Lodge of Oz seemed to be the right place for us to be. It had a magical feel, like the welcome warmth of home, even though it was a company. I feel home is where your heart is and Tommy and my home was with each other wherever we were.

We had our own 'apartment' like room. It had a living area, bedroom and bathroom. There was a shared kitchen where each resident had their own cabinets, and a designated spot in the fridge. This was where we met many of our soon to be friends.

We had learned a game of dominoes called Chicken foot.

Playing dominos at Hope Lodge

We'd go to the dining room to play the game, then we noticed everyone's interest in the game. It was so satisfying to know that when we got to the Lodge, most of the residents were segregated, or wanting to stay in their own little area. Chicken foot brought everyone together. We bought several sets of dominoes and we'd all sit around the dining room together and play, laugh and be together.

It brought smiles to faces because now the folks suffering had something else to think of beside their illness. It was nice to have been part of their joy.

Tommy started his radiation at Shands and it caused him to feel nauseated. However, once he lay down for a while, he'd start feeling better so he'd get up and go to check on our friends, in our now new gathering place, the dining area.

I want to tell you about one special girl. Her name was Danielle and her grandmother was battling cancer. Danielle was staying with her grandma at the Lodge and I found out the young lady was about to celebrate her sixteenth birthday.

We decided to throw her a surprise sweet sixteen party. She was in to Mickey Mouse, so the décor and gifts were easy to buy. Danielle was *so* surprised.

It was a good time all around. Tommy had a way about him. He could always get folks laughing and talking. He did a lot to brighten the atmosphere for all those suffering. That day gave everyone a glimpse of family.

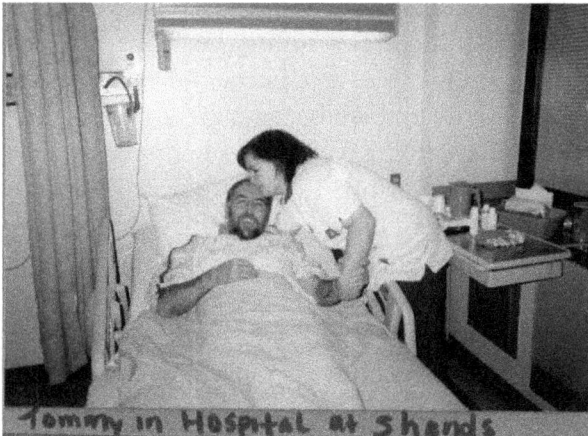
Danielle's Birthday

Tommy in Hospital at Shands

Forrest Gump was the rage movie at the time, and Tommy loved it. He could relate to the plot because of the part about the Vietnam war. Sometimes Tommy would act just like Forrest and it made me laugh.

Treatments over, it was time for us to leave the lodge and go to stay with Tommy's family. We got out our address book and got names and numbers of all of our friends. Vowing to keep in touch, it was time to depart.

My friend Judy didn't want to see us go. She said we were good for moral. It was hard to keep the moral up when so many of those who surrounded us had already made their journey to the kingdom of Heaven.

There were reunions of those who were still living. One year at Christmas, Tommy played Santa at the Shands hospital. People donated gifts for the children there. Then after he'd given out the gifts, we went to the Lodge, knowing the residents couldn't leave to go home to their families for the holiday.

I worked at the Golden Corral at the time and they were kind enough to donate food for a special Christmas feast at the Hope lodge of Oz. It was a special evening I'll never forget.

I'd taken my karaoke machine so we could all sing Christmas songs, but I had laryngitis and was having a really hard time singing. A nice gentleman, from a different country, was one of the patients. He stood up and made his way over to me. He was a big man with very kind eyes.

He asked if he could be of assistance. I told him sure! So he took the microphone from me and began to sing. He had such a beautiful baritone voice everyone just stared at him in awe. I found out later he was an opera singer. There was no doubt in my mind he had a God given talent.

Amazing singer

Our Hope Lodge of Oz will always hold a place in my heart. I'll be forever grateful to the loving staff. When we left, we bought some statues to decorate the beautiful courtyard called The Angel's Sanctuary of Hope. They would symbolize the safe haven of the Lodge and portray the angels that worked there.

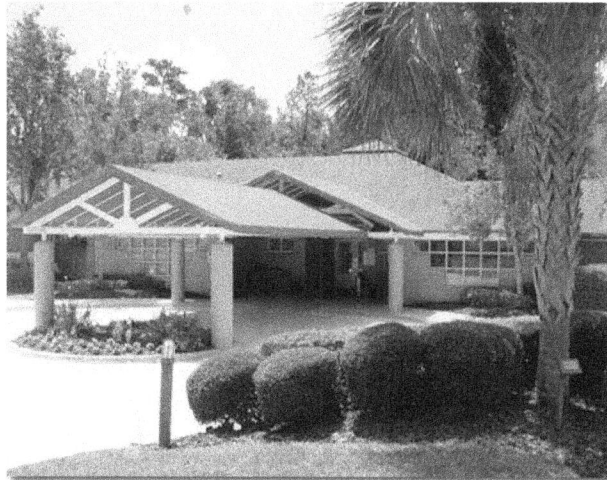

April 29, 2002

Dear Tom and Sheree,

You are just two amazing people! Thank you so much for your gifts. The birdbath is in the garden near the dry creek bed and the gazebo. It is by far the cutest one I've ever seen and looks like it was made with our garden in mind. The beautiful angel is tucked in a nook — a kind of surprise for folks strolling through the garden.

I'll send pictures soon. Thank you again. It was just great seeing you at Homecoming.

Fondly,
Judy

I think it's ironic that we got this letter from Judy in April 2002. Tommy was cancer free until 2002. Then the tornado returned.

The Storm

This time life changes

It was the day after Christmas, in 2002. Tommy and I lived in Jacksonville, Florida. We bought a house. We'd been living in a rental after his testicular cancer.

I finally got the waitress job I wanted at Golden Corral. It was such a nice place to work. Even though I loved my job, I realized that sometimes you have to overlook the obstacles in your path. The emotions you deal with when you know the love of your life has gone through so much, is almost more than you can bear. You wonder how much more can one take. However you try to make a living and support the best you can, while going through tough times.

That particular day I got off work, and like always, Tommy came to pick me up. He had our evening meal ready. It was leftovers from Christmas dinner, my favorite, turkey and dressing with all the trimmings.

We sat down to eat and the doorbell rang. The neighbor from across the street needed help, so off Tommy went. When he came back home he went to the kitchen, then came into the living room. He was unstable walking and said he had trouble seeing, so I had him sit in his chair.

Then out of nowhere, he said, "Help me! Help me, please."

That really lit a fire under my heels. Never did he ask in such a way for help. It alarmed me, so I called for Glen, his Vietnam buddy that lived behind us.

I knew Tommy would have to go to the hospital, so I got him ready. When Glen got to our house, I asked him drive our van to take us because I was too shaky. He agreed and off we went to the civilian hospital down town in Jacksonville.

There Tommy was brought a wheelchair, and I had Glen, after a while go, back home to check on our cocker spaniels. I told him, I would call him. When I wanted to go back to where Tommy was taken, and they wouldn't let me, I said possible stroke, I read of the warning signs.

After a long while I was able to go back and be with Tommy. There he was tied down, and he had a neck brace on, they said, he was unattended and fell off the gurney, and landed on the floor. Then, he had several holding him down on table, seizures, and they cut off his clothes, and his personal belongings were scattered all over the floor. I was really mad!

He went through this without me being allowed back there, I could have stayed with him and protected him. They ended up admitting him in the hospital. I called his family. After a week, Tommy was able to come home. If they ran tests, possible stroke/seizures. Then I decided to get another opinion, because Tommy was not any better. So I drove him to Gainesville, Florida, one and a half hours away and had took him to VA, and since he didn't have an appointment—They made us sit in waiting area, 7 a.m. until 3 p.m. I was fit to be tied—I was so upset, and crying, and it was so hard for Tommy to just sit there.

I know I made a scene, and they finally called his name, they wouldn't let me go back with him. So they ended up putting me into a room by myself. It seemed like forever, they finally ran all tests, and then we had to get release papers, then they said they would call when they got results.

Those times were so hard!! I was trying to work full time, and worried about him, being alone at home. I had neighbors and friends, and family checking up on him. In between all this there was this manager, and he was making it hard on me, I didn't miss any work, but he didn't like me, and that's another story—later I found out he no longer employed there because, as much as I hated to, I couldn't deal with that, *and* all I was going through with my Tommy, so I went to work at another place. I waitressed, but tips were bad! Hard to make a living to support family, but couldn't worry about that just then, I had to focus on Tommy.

Well, it was a couple of days, and received a phone call VA wanted us to bring family, and they wanted to talk to us. Then we were scared! And God! I prayed so hard, like I always had, but this time I needed God.

Please I prayed. *Keep me strong, and help Tommy*. Well, we all arrived there at Shands/VA. The doctor came into the room; we could tell this wasn't going to turn out well.

He went over to Tommy, then proceeded to tell him, "You need to get your affairs in order. You have Glioblastoma Multiform, malignant brain cancer. I'm sorry, but it's stage four. You have only two months to live."

I was devastated. I felt my world was ending, but I kept listening as he talked about the options, to operate, to prolong, but my Tommy was going to die. He couldn't!

I was beside Tommy holding his hand when he started to cry. I cried with him, holding him, God! Please help me! I felt so sad for Tommy. He was in shock, we all were in shock. The news shocked him.

I knew I had to be strong for Tommy, but I didn't want to lose him, being without my best friend, all we have been through. The surgery was Valentine's day, and since being close to my birthday, my girlfriends from work wanted to take me out, and I said no. I want to be close in case Tommy needs me.

I settled for Shands cafeteria, but told them where I could be reached. I really wasn't hungry, I wasn't thinking about that.

One of my friends said, "But, Sheree, your stomachs growling, tells us differently."

I couldn't think about myself! I know my friends, as always, had good intentions.

When Tommy had been better, sometimes we all went out dancing, and the cancer walk, and the nursing home for Christmas, Tommy being Santa, and all that, they liked him, and wanted to be there for me.

So much Love, I was fortunate to have their devotion. I was called back to recovery, and one of my girlfriends came with me.

Tommy was waking up, and he said, "Tiger, did you get your gifts?"

I started to say I didn't care, but my friend nudged me and said, "Sheree, he just woke up out of brain surgery, and you were the first person on his mind."

So I said, "Honey, I haven't been home, but that was thoughtful for you to remember my Valentines, and my birthday." But that was the kind of sweetheart Tommy was.

This was a Valentine's Day some years before.

I would do whatever it took, wherever I was to journey, and cherish whenever the time would be to be by his side. Because I knew in a heartbeat, he would do it and more for me. That is when you truly love someone.

I had finally met my knight in shining armor, after being with so many bad ones, self-absorbed, mean and hurtful! Tommy was my ray of sunshine! My, *glad and thankful to be with you*, kind of man. I was a free spirit, and there seemed to be nothing ever keeping us from our love for each other.

We had almost 17 years of roller coaster rides, of life. One thing you learn, the materialistic items in life can be replaced, but having someone that genuinely loves you, and accepts you for yourself; who doesn't try to change you, well, that is the best feeling I have ever had.

To know that Tommy loved me is all I ever wanted. To be loved and cared for. It is so nice to lie beside Tommy and know when he hugged me and got close, the warmth of his love and touch, his embrace, to hear his heartbeat, sleeping is so sweet!

Tommy had a gentle touch, but was so strong. When he laughed you just had to laugh right along with him. His smile, along with his bright blue eyes, illumined his personality. However, during those days the thoughts of Tommy's ways kept me strong! And God in my life, everyday prayers, helped me get through the toughest times! And unknowingly, I was about to experience in the days ahead.

Tommy after surgery 2003

At Hospice

The Journey Home to God

Tommy and I tried to live our lives as normal as we could. I would go to work, and he was busy around the house. But now there were the caregivers. Family and friends helped out as much as possible, and so thankful for all their love and support.

Everyone loved Tommy. I don't think he ever met a stranger. Tommy always welcomed, talked to make you feel you knew him for a long time, but only for a while. We had homecare Hospice, set up for us.

Our home, they brought a bed and all medical equipment needed. Then all the meds, and when to take, that had to be on a chart—and Tommy's sister and caregivers helped with that.

A few weeks prior, I was at work, so Tommy's sister and husband wanted to pick up Tommy and go to see a movie. They had good intentions, but I received a phone call at work. Tommy was at Orange Park Medical Center. He had a seizure in the theater, and they had to stop the movie, turn on the lights, and ask if there was a doctor or someone to help Tommy.

I got to the hospital, family came and picked me up, and Tommy was having several seizures, one after the other. They admitted him into the hospital there he stayed for several days. I later found out, that the theater was crowded, and Tommy ended up sitting alone. I was really upset!

This was a crucial time for Tommy and crowds were neither what he needed, nor sitting alone with strangers. But I held it in because I didn't want any added stress!

Tommy's sister talked me into getting a cell phone, because of Tommy and I had gotten one, I really didn't have it in me to work, but I knew there were bills to pay, and life supposedly went on. I was always responsible. I never miss work, and I focused on my job, no matter at so many trying times it was really hard! But I prayed to God to give me strength, and to please support and comfort, and protect my Tommy.

Tommy came back home from the hospital. I think they had to get his meds leveled. It came to the day when he no longer would take his meds by mouth. They told me I would have to give them up his hind quarters. OH! My God! I tried so hard, but Tommy would yell out in pain, and I was shaking and I didn't want to hurt him. I loved him.

Then hospice homecare was over, the decision to ambulatory him to the hospice center came soon. When we arrived there they took us to the other side of building and gave him a room. Then it wasn't long after that, they said, wrong room, and took us to another part of the building, gave him a room and soon they set me up with a cot.

I am so thankful for all my family and friends that helped with my cocker spaniels, Gomer and Patches, they were our babies and Tommy's company when I was at work. I tried to work, running back and forth, but I was so afraid that Tommy would die, and I wouldn't get to see him.

One day at work the waitresses, along with some managers, and they all were around customers, my friends I have known for some time gave me a card, and inside the envelope was money they all gave me and told me, you don't need to be at work, you need to be with Tommy. I started crying, couldn't stop, but I felt a sense of relief, because now I could be with Tommy where my Heart wanted to be. I thanked them ever so much and hugged each one.

I can't tell you what this means to me, I was totally touched! I went home and friends took care of house and babies so I packed a bag and off I went to be with Tommy. I slept with Tommy's favorite throw, the American Flag on me, and Tommy had it on him when we wheel-chaired him around the gardens.

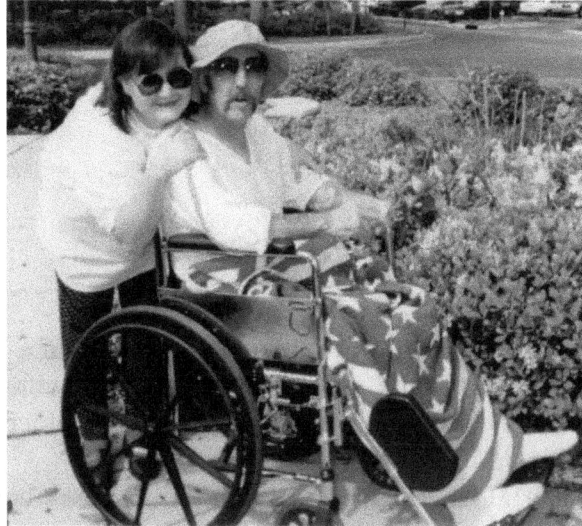

Sheree wheeling Tommy in the Hospice gardens

It was springtime, and the flowers were in bloom with their fragrance perfumes and the birds were singing, flying almost gliding from one branch to another.

They had benches, and a gazebo, and that's where Tommy liked sitting in his wheelchair—There we had our memories. Tommy told me he loved me so many times.

"Tiger, thank you! For being my wife, for taking care of me for staying with me, for never giving up on me!"

I would always start to cry. I would have to control myself, because things were always hard enough for him.

His family would guide him in his wheelchair, I would walk by his side, and he always wanted to stop in the Chapel. I feel that gave him a sense of peace, his connection with God and the comfort Tommy felt being closer to God.

The stain glass windows, and the altar, then one day Tommy told us, that he wanted his celebration of life in the chapel, this one. We all said alright! If that's what you want. Then I hugged his neck and kissed him. As much as I cried, I know those words somehow even comforted me. At the same token, I didn't want to think ahead. Just live out every moment, because that's all we had right then together.

Then by some miracle a red bird came pecking on Tommy's window pane, three days in a row. And always around the same time so after seeing it the first day, I went with Brandi, Tommy's sister, and we went to the store and I got him a feeder, and a statue of an angel with a little boy holding a lantern with a candle inside.

I felt in my heart Tommy needed that statue, so beautiful, and so meaningful! I had the hospice folks place the feeder outside in front of his window and the statue in front of Tommy's bed, right on the cabinet, so he could see the angel and share the light of comfort.

I felt that the red bird's visits were a sign from God that the time was growing near. Soon Tommy was unable to get out of bed, he was pulling out his tubes and he was going blind. That man that I loved, soon wouldn't be Tommy anymore.

The brain cancer was taking him away, and his body was shutting down. I was glad that while

Tommy could still see, he got to see his babies Gomer and Patches. He loved them so much. Glen was very nice to bring them, they were a major part of our family, and I know they had wondered where their daddy was.

Patches and Gomer

Then the family came up, one day spent time with me and his brother, Barry stayed with Tommy in his room. It got there toward evening, Tommy's sister had me busy with a puzzle, and it was around 8:30 p.m. when Barry came out of the room. The look on his face concerned me.

"Tommy has gone to be with God!"

We went to say 'see you later'. I hated good-bye, such a final word, not a happy one, always felt so sad!

After my final parting with the man I loved, the family helped me with my belongings. I felt from then on I just was going through the motions. I stayed with them in one of their bedrooms, but I so wanted to go home and be with my babies.

I felt hollow, full of loss and despair! I was alone and I couldn't stop crying! My emotions came pouring out, I felt drained and dull. I was going through depression, and it was hurting so bad!

God, I need you ever so much! Did my Tommy arrive there, please give him wings so he can fly to lay beside me in our bed.

It was so big and empty. I wrapped my arms around his pillow, and covered myself with his blanket. I could still smell him, and I saw his clothes hanging in the closet. All the items in the house were about us…together. The days ahead were some of the hardest.

Tommy's Love Letter to Me

His final farewell

Before his death Tommy had a lot on his mind, and most of that was about me. As much as I wanted him to take that time to think about himself, that wasn't Tommy. I was the center of his world, and he will always be mine!

He wanted me to learn everything about the house that I would need to know—a crash course, say as you will, on survival, a widow's survival. I didn't have it in me to go through all the knowledge of the air-conditioning, the oil in the van, the fire extinguisher, repairs on house—I didn't feel I wanted to know. I had him; he did all that was needed…but now, he was gone.

A friend told me, she had a vision—and Tommy was in Heaven. There was an archway, trellis, flowers, and a beautiful lady with long flowing hair (by pictures that must have been Tommy's mother) and his grandfather then Barney and Thelma, our cocker spaniels. She said he walked with them all through the trellis, and into Heaven.

That somehow gave me the peace in my heart and soul I needed to sustain my existence then. I felt I was going through the motions. If it weren't for family and friends, I couldn't have endured these heart pressing times. There was a service to plan, things to arrange, and friends and family to attend—and share with us—all about Tommy. It was time for me to go home.

When I came home finally after staying with Tommy's sister, I went into the office, the last room we fixed up and Tommy had it looking so nice! I felt his presence so warm and loving—then I looked in bottom of the desk drawer, and there was this white envelope that had my nickname 'Tiger' written in his hand. I opened the envelope and when I pulled out the paper inside, I realized it was a love letter.

I shared with others what my Tommy had written to them. For me, he covered everything—that I should do. *Don't let no one take advantage of you, not anymore.* God gave to me Tommy, and I have been so blessed and loved by knowing such a kind, thoughtful, considerate, unselfish man.

I have never in my whole life experienced the love I felt when I had him. And I still do have him in my heart my memories, and always will because Tommy is so much a part of me.

Every day, I live my life he is always by my side—people might think I am off my rocker, but they don't know about my Tommy. I talk to him or a song reminds me of him, and I smile or shed a tear. Whatever I feel, it's my right!

Here's part of the letter in his own hand writing.

iN CASE things don't work out AS PLANNE
Do me A Javor give Body Away To Science ①
Let them see where things went wrong
Thank you Jor Being the Best wife Anyman could
ever hope To have or ever Ask Jor don't Be
Sad we were Lucky more than Some we had
19 BeauJul years sure we had Rough Times
But thats Life our Love was the Best, You Are
the hardest worker I Ever knew give my clothes
Away Jirst things To Some one you can get Some
use out of them Remember harder small the
Longer you keep ALL this the harder it is. we
Both know this better than most Re lo the office
this is what I want it's not much to Ask keep
VA Jiles & SS Jiles Jor money purposes
my pictures with you you can keep.

ALL our dreams came true Look AhL the things
we have done places we have been wemove
the house Look Nice But now its time to move
on Life goes on you have to now help your

(15)

Don't do Like me there are more than
Bills in Life Live in the momment
Take time For Fun in your Life

I Love you all get A Lot to do
in A short time and these pages are
not easy For me to write I was Lucky
I had a good Bic pen and some thick
Towels For Tears gotto go Have
A Lot to get done

Remember don't Live in the
Past I am gone and my Life
is over But not yours Have
Fun And Live in the momoment
Cut down on stress I didn't
See what happened
Don't cry For me I am in A better place
I will be ok Live For the moment
Thank you all For Being A part of my
Life And making it a better place
gotto go I think they are Calling my
No ha, ha, Take care Love Tommy

35

(16)

How you like my short N.

Hey you know me And my Books
Just want to thank you All
One more time For the memories
And the laughs we All shared

I will miss you All And you
All will Be in ...
          I Love you All very
     much. Love Tom

I knew All Along that this was
the end My Luck had Run out
but I thank you All For All you
had done For me And All your prayers

     I will miss you All
          Love Tom

     Take Core Sheree you are
     A strong girl You gift Are in
     the Bottom Draw Just As you
          Walk in Room white cAbinet
I Love you honey But you must must
Move on.

Then soon was his service.

Tommy's Celebration of Life

Hospice Chapel

We had been working for several days to make Tommy's celebration one that would always remember. To include an arrangement of photos, thanks to Tommy's brother-in-law, JD who captured all that is good with Tommy's eyes, his smile and laughter with family and friends.

Photos of Tommy when he was a baby, then through his growing up years, were placed perfectly on the altar along with photo albums, an angel that had optics glowing, changing iridescent colors, a wishing well, a dove, a butterfly and dragonfly. I know Tommy was there, shining his light for others to see.

We worked on a pamphlet to have at the service, all about Tommy. I am honored to share with those to feel some sense of Tommy's aura—his spiritual angelic, magical presence. The day came for Tommy's celebration of his life—and the chapel at Hospice, filled up and had to go get more chairs because so many cared and loved Tommy, looked perfect.

Not only were family and close friends in attendance, but customers from work and even his dentist. I looked around and knew Tommy would like what he saw. He was a humble man. How could he know so many adored him?

He never felt he was a better man, a wealthy man, but he was. He had something totally unbelievable, that any other would just be envious, he had a circle of Love, true to himself, we loved him just the way he was—a marine veteran, fought in Vietnam, survived, wounded twice, two Purple Hearts, and a man with valor, and pride and dignity. Family and friends one by one talked in front about knowing Tommy and being a part of his life.

Then, after the service, we went into the courtyard where we released balloons to go up to Heaven for Tommy—and I wrote my poem for him, and I will share with you the following—Because it is not a final farewell, it's the beginning of a forever kind of relationship I have knowing that Tommy will be with me until god calls me home, so I can be with him once again!

Once we were finished, and all was over, we drove over to the restaurant I was working at , and we shared each other's friendship at the table, with God's Blessings, to finish our Celebration—For Tommy, and the Joy and Memories he gave each of us. I felt so lucky and fortunate to have so many family and friends that shared with me Tommy's Day!

My Poem...

Tommy Can You Hear Me?

Tommy, can you hear me calling your name
Can you feel my heartbeat
Do you know I miss you time and again

Tommy, can you see me planting your flower
Oh! What a beautiful landscape
And the birds singing & resting
Oh! So sweetly

Tommy, can I touch you, feel your love
And your warm embrace
How I long for your love

Tommy, please stay near me, never drift away
Send me a sign, like a butterfly, a blooming rose
The wind, whispering your love

Tommy, I will always love you
You will be in my heart forever
Locked away, and for you, my love will stay
Lover, Wife & Soul Mate

Tiger,
Sheree

Dance, Express yourself

Spiritual Intervention

At the lowest peak after the loss of Tommy, I prayed for guidance, and reassurance about where I was headed. I thought I wanted to keep our house in Florida, but something was calling me to go back home to Springfield, MO. I missed the four seasons.

Don't get me wrong, the ocean was nothing to sneeze about, hearing the sounds of the waves, the birds and seagulls were refreshing. Feeling the warmth of the sun and being barefooted in the sand's silky texture was nice, but I enjoyed doing those things with Tommy. Now it just wasn't the same.

I recalled the days we flew kites, or took out bicycles to ride, threw crackers up in the air for gulls, or just rested on the beach on a blanket and watched the waves as they came rolling in. That was a special chapter in my life. Something I can hold close to my heart and treasure for all it gives me! But I knew things were to be as I would have them.

Just like the wind changes so did my existence. I felt closer to God in prayer. Throughout these days I received great comfort when I felt His presence, and the calling of angels to protect me as my journey through life moved forward.

Then came God's spiritual intervention and I felt Tommy had a big part of guiding me onward. God and Tommy knew I needed something or someone in my life that I wasn't going to find in Florida.

I made reservations to fly back home, get a rental car, and to book a motel room. I had never in my life, done that before, and it felt scary, but at the same time, I knew it was something I needed to do.

I think I had angel Tommy guiding me along with every step, giving me courage to handle my life as best I could. I reached Springfield and I glancing down before landing I looked out the window of the plane, and saw the rolling hills, the beautiful landscape, the cows, farms and crops. It truly is a place made by God's hands.

Springtime is so glorious with everything budding and starting to turn green, while wakening up from cold, dark still winter's nap. We landed at the airport, and I got my luggage, then went to find the place I made reservations for the rental car. When I first made reservations for the car I wanted a white Toyota Corolla with a cd player, and they said they didn't have one. I was going to have to settle another model in a different color. I said okay as long as there was a cd player, because I needed my music.

Hearing happy voices helped me, gave life to my inner spirit, because with Tommy I always loved to dance. We did alone or out with our friends. And inside of me, it flowed like blood through my veins.

Well, when I went over to the rental desk the lady, asked for my name, and told me—the car was parked out in the front lot. Guess what, it was a white Toyota Corolla. Wow! I didn't think I was going to get that one. Truly Amazing! That was a miracle for me.

She handed me the keys and with my luggage I was off to the car. I unlocked it and got in then drove it away. So exciting! I got a map before because it has been some years since being home. I found the motel, nothing fancy, just like me, down to Earth. I went into the front desk, got my key card then parked on the other side. I unloaded everything then collapsed on the bed. I was exhausted.

The next day I went around and visited my relatives even my mom and her boyfriend. I took them out to eat. My mom said that I needed to come back and visit again. I told her I might if I had the time. I visited my middle sister, and we talked and talked.

I left, went back to motel room. I called my brother up that's 13 months older than me and we made arrangements to go out dancing at a place I have never been. Of course, I didn't know that town's activities. So I went to eat, and then drove over to the place.

He was supposed to meet me there, then said he had to work over. I waited and waited. I was all alone and didn't know any one. Scary! The music was playing and I was drinking, and I smoked a cigarette, I had previously been around my sister and she smoked, though I really didn't smoke that time it helped me relax.

A song started and there were a few getting up to go to the dance floor. Then I saw this guy. He had dark hair and wore a cowboy hat. He was dancing alone on floor.

I told myself, *well, if he can do it, so can you! Be brave you can get up there. you don't need a dance partner.*

Then I did it, but it hit me that this was the first time I had danced without Tommy and I went over to sit down. Tears started to flow, but I told myself, *try and smile and be happy, If not for myself remember the love letter Tommy wrote. Don't cry, be happy!*

I felt Tommy with me. And I heard his voice, as I did through my whole trip. The song was over and the cowboy came over, and asked if I wanted to dance. Something inside of me was telling me it was alright! So I agreed. We danced to one song then we danced again!

The place was getting packed. He came over to tell me he was leaving, I had been drinking a few, and it was so loud. He asked me if I would be there Friday or Saturday, and I said Friday, and he left. Now I was alone again!

I stayed close to the bar and when they were closing, I walked out the door, and went to the rental car. I opened the door and sat just sat there. I realized then I couldn't drive this way, and I started to cry, sobbing, uncontrollable. What was I going to do?

Then another miracle happened. A bunch of girls came over to me. One girl started asking, "Why are you crying?"

I told her about Tommy.

She took my car keys out of my hand, and said, "You are going with us!"

I asked, "What about the car!"

She replied, "We will leave it locked up for now. You could be my mother, and I wouldn't leave her alone, crying."

So I went with them, and I remember someone holding my hand and another one hugging me. I woke up the next day and saw a bunch of beds. I recognized the familiar face of the girl that talked to me in the car. She was in the bed next to where I was sleeping.

I went over to her and I woke her up. "I am sorry! But where am I?" I was scared.

"You're okay. You're in the SMS dormitory for girls."

WOW! I thought. I'd never been in a dorm before. There were a lot of beds. I asked her if she could take me to get the car when she could. So she said okay. Let me get dressed. And I thanked her, must have been a thousand times.

And I got my shoes, and purse, and we left. She dropped me off to where the car was, and I offered her money, and she wouldn't take it! She was so sweet and her voice was so kind. I drove to my motel room and collapsed on bed.

I started to cry, and I thanked God for sending His angels to protect me. I promised myself that I wouldn't go anywhere I wouldn't leave that room. I was embarrassed but so grateful! I prayed to God, and Tommy, I was so sorry for not being responsible.

I let my emotions get the best of me! I was missing Tommy so much! And being alone was all new to me. I knew I couldn't just stay in that room forever even if it was what I wanted to do. I prayed that

Tommy would give me a sign.

Well, then my brother called and asked if I wanted to go to the dance hall on Friday night. I briefly thought of the cowboy I'd seen there before. I agreed so we met. It was good to see my brother, his wife, their daughter and her husband, but when the cowboy walked up, it was good to see him, too. His dark hair was shining he smiled and his eyes just glowed. I felt like a school girl on her first date.

I introduced him to my family. All I knew at that time was his first name was David, and he sat down to visit. We talked about our lives. I told him about Tommy, and he told me that his mom died from brain tumor and he was real close to her. And we talked for a while then we went to dance. The song, I'm proud to be an American by Lee Greenwood started to play. That was Tommy's favorite song.

The cowboy and I just stood there, then right behind us the American flag came down from the ceiling. I turned and started to cry. Oh, my God, Tommy was sending the sign I'd asked for. I felt it in my heart. God and Tommy sent the man standing next to me too be my friend.

At the end of the night we went for breakfast talked until he had to get back to the farm. David was staying at an older man's farm, helping to watch and take care of what he could.

He asked me out to dinner and I said yes. That night there were a few more signs that this may lead to a new chapter in my life. I told him about the nickname Tommy gave me, Tiger. He told me his dad called him Tiger when he was a boy. Then I told him Tommy had a couple of Purple Hearts, and his tag number was 007, he was always proud of that! David showed me the last three numbers of his social. Really? 007. WOW!

From that day on we've remained friends because those truly were signs from God and Tommy. Tommy was letting me know it was alright to have a special friend and I believe he sent him to me. My husband knew I'd need a kind and caring man, like he was, to help me though life without him. And David is that man.

I decided to move back to Missouri.

My Battle

Remember the Promise

After I moved from Florida back home to Missouri, with David's help I found a house and settled in. Then I got started on what I promised Tommy about, The Fight to Make It Right!

I needed to try to get my DIC (Dependency and Indemnity Compensation) widows pension. But I knew it would be hard after all those years of him going back and forth to VA, and them trying to cover up what they knew was going on (poisoning from Agent Orange).

The ones in charge should be ashamed of themselves! What would Jesus think if He was here to witness their wrong! But they forget God is everywhere, every day. He created such a beautiful world! One He didn't intend for Man to ruin it by all the senseless power games.

To use horrible life-taking, slow killing toxic chemicals and spray it on our own men, who were trying to stay alive in battle was a heresy.

God watches while others destroy so many lives and our planet. May God have mercy on those responsible souls from the Vietnam era! To try and deny that they knew what hazardous effects the poison caused to so many.

The trouble is I think and feel the medics in the field didn't know the first thing about naming certain ailments. They weren't trained to know and no one bothered to tell them. They just used what they knew and made a judgment call.

Trained personnel are the ones that covered it up! Not once thinking or caring what harmful effects it caused on our men! Their men.

For me, it took away the love of my life. Such a heroic man that gave to me his all! We were a team, a perfect circle, just like the gold bands we wore on our fingers.

The full first year I lived in Missouri, David helped support me I didn't have work at a regular job. I could focus on gathering all of the files I would need to prove what Tommy and I had gone through over the years. Believe me, that task in itself was a full time job.

Even before we were together, when he was in the Military, Tommy had kept a bunch of boxes of paperwork, medical records and paperwork proving that he suffered from Agent Orange. I sifted through it, made copies and put the originals away for safe keeping.

I tried to take all of the names/wording/symptoms of any cancers I could find and match them up with his medical records. The computer was a lot of help in this quest. That was only part of what I did, but I will say that several matched.

Organizations I got involved with also helped me in my quest. They are mentioned later along with their organization information.

Once I got the ball rolling, I decided it was time to get a job.

I didn't want to waitress anymore. I did it for 31 years. It was time to try something new. I put in application at a well-known retail store newly built in my home town. After that, I went to visit my Aunt and Uncle in Kansas. That's where I got the phone call that I was hired.

Once I went to work I learned a lot, made new friends, prayed thanks to God for blessing me with a job.

I worked hard, never called in, I was never late, and always did what I was told. However, working a fulltime job, with its ups and downs, took its toll on my mind and body.

I hired the law firm of Bergmann & Moore, LLC. This is one of the letters I received from them.

Bergmann & Moore, LLC

Joseph R. Moore, Esq.
Partner

Glenn R. Bergmann, Esq.
Partner

Sent Via First Class Mail

August 12, 2009

Ms. Sheree E Evans
1504 West Daniels Street
Ozark, MO 65721

Dear Ms. Evans:

By now, I am sure that you are very familiar with the range and level of service that we at Bergmann and Moore have to offer. We continue to tirelessly fight for your VA benefits and the benefits of many others like you before the VA.

We are a growing law firm still devoted exclusively to fighting for veterans' claims before the VA. We have successfully helped countless veterans and widows win their cases and get the benefits that they rightfully deserve. Still, there are many out there who may be confused by the VA process or who just want to give up after fighting for so long. As I am sure you can attest to, the VA process is both stressful and time-consuming. We want to make sure that every individual who deserves benefits from the VA gets what is justifiably theirs, especially in this tough economic climate. Having an attorney with firsthand knowledge of the process helps ensure that claims are dealt with correctly and promptly.

We have included some business cards. If you know other individuals in your situation who you think could benefit from our services, please feel free to give them a card (when they call us, make sure to tell them to use your name—we get a lot of calls, and we want to make sure we take care of our friends first). If you ever need more cards, please let us know.

Sincerely,

Joseph R. Moore, Esq.
Bergmann & Moore, LLC

Glenn R. Bergmann, Esq.
Bergmann & Moore, LLC

While fighting for my widow's pension, I broke out in whelps and hurt so bad! My nerves were getting the best of me, but I kept praying it would all get better. God was always there to guide me, to protect me.

I had two living things left from when Tommy was alive. Patches and Gomer. They were getting up in age and my heart broke when the first to go after Tommy, was Patches. Gomer was all I had left. At fourteen years old, he passed from congestive heart failure and joined Patches and Tommy in Heaven. Thank God for David.

I did a lot of research and the computer was my best friend. God gave me the stepping stones to get what I needed done! To trust you can achieve and reach your goals if very important. You just have to believe in yourself, and know that anything is possible! I realized that, when over the next few years I fought many health issues myself while at the same time, working on my case.

My case also kept my mind occupied. It took me eight years to win, but it was worth it. My documentation you'll see later in the pages of this book.

Quarters from Heaven

Signs

I was working diligently on the case to prove Agent Orange caused Tommy's death. Hour upon hour, I spent doing research. But one week in particular I seemed to be working harder than ever.

In my explorations I found out The Agent Orange Act 1991 law was passed in February of that year. This act was the first to grant presumptive benefits. See below

```
Agent Orange Act of 1991 Pub. L. 102-4 (1991)



        PUBLIC LAW 102-4- FEB. 6, 1991        105 STAT 11

Public Law 102-4
102d Congress
                                      Feb. 6, 1991
                                      (H.R. 555)


                   An Act

To provide for the Secretary of Veterans Affairs to obtain
independent scientific review of the available scientific
evidence regarding associations between diseases and exposure
to dioxim and other chemical compounds in herbicides, and for
other purposes.

    Be it enacted by the Senate and House of Representatives of
the United States of America in Congress assembled,

SECTION 1.  SHORT TITLE.                 Agent Orange
    This Act may be cited as the "Agent Orange    Act of 1991
    Act of 1991"                         88 USC 101 code.

SEC. 2 PRESUMPTION OF SERVICE CONNECTION FOR DISEASES
       ASSOCIATED WITH EXPOSURE TO CERTAIN HERBICIDE AGENTS.

   (a)  IN GENERAL. - (1)  Chapter II of title 88, United States
Code, is amended by adding at the end of subchapter II the
following new section:

" 316.  Presumptions of service connection for disease associated
        with exposure to certain herbicide agents.
```

See the complete law at:
http://www2.gwu.edu/~nsarchiv/radiation/dir/mstreet/commeet/meet3/brief3.gfr/tab_g/br3g1f.txt

The date of Tommy's first cancer, the Testicular cancer was in 1994. 1991 and 1994. For some reason, those dates stuck in my head. I thought about them all week.

That same week, every evening after I got off work at the store, it seemed I needed to buy something to take home. Each night I would go through a different checkout line. I always paid with cash and put the change in my purse. After I'd get home I looked at my change because I saved coins. I was always looking for those quarters from each state.

The first night, I looked at the head side of the quarter and it had the date 1991 on it. That years date was etched in my mind because of the Agent Orange Act. I knew the state quarters didn't come out until 1999, so this wasn't one of them. However, something compelled me to look at the tale side of the coin. My pulse quickened when I turned it over and saw another head. Wow! A two-headed quarter. I'd never seen one before. Odd.

Another night that same week…déjà Vu. After work I went through another line to purchase my goods and as always, I looked through my change when I get home. I studied the coins and oh my gosh, there I was gazing at 1994 quarter. The year of Tommy's first cancer. It wasn't one I would put in my state quarter collection either, but for some reason I wanted to keep it anyway. I turned it over to look at the other side and my jaw dropped. It couldn't be! Another two headed quarter. This was unbelievable!

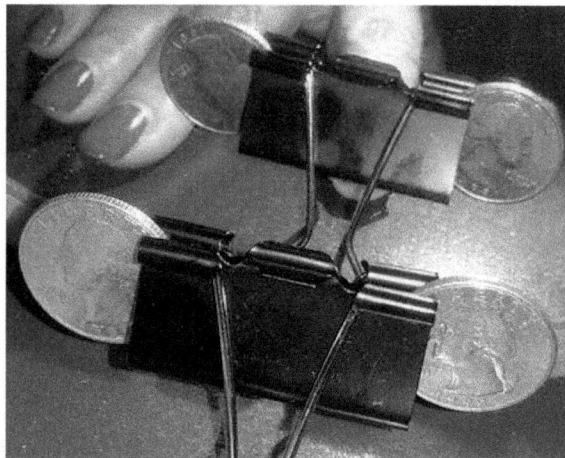

Picture of the actual quarters.

What are the chances that something as unique as that happening? Both in the same week. The week I'd worked harder than ever on my case.

These were signs. Angels, Tommy, Messengers of God, were guiding me. I felt I must have been on the right track in the work I was doing in Tommy's memory, and for my case. I truly felt in my heart, blessed to have such a strong bond with my husband that he would let me know I was doing the right thing.

The Final Chapter

By the Grace of God, A Promise Kept

I'll never forget the 27th day of January 2011.

Burr! It was cold, cloudy day. To me January is a calm, quiet month to reflect on everything being still, kind of stagnant in time. But outside there's a fresh, crispness in the air. You have something to look forward to because you know Spring is around the corner.

I had started getting ready for work but didn't have to be thee until 2 p.m. My cell phone rang. I went to pick it up and my lawyer Glenn Bergmann was on the other end. His voice rang through the speaker.

"Are you sitting down?"

"No, but I will." I thought that was a peculiar way to start a conversation. I took a seat and held my breath. "Okay, I'm sitting."

He then said very loud and clear. "You won!"

I couldn't believe what I'd just heard. My heart jumped to my throat. "What?!"

He said, "You won, your DIC Widows pension!" In a somewhat calmer voice he added, "It's all over. Congratulations!"

I let out the breath I'd been holding. Finally, after 8 years, it was over. Was this too good to be true?! I had to be positive. "Are you sure?" I was so used to them denying, it was hard to grasp.

"No, Sheree Evans, once they award the final decision, they can't go back…ever! Case is closed, finished!"

Then I started crying. All emotions flooded through my being. I then told him, "Thank you! So much!"

He said, "You did all the paperwork and detailed research. We handled the legal end."

Then I silently thanked God for answering my prayers and helping me through such difficult hard time.

I felt as if tons of bricks were lifted off my shoulders. I could breathe, exhale! I was crying tears of happiness! I had made a promise to Tommy at Hospice, and I was able to keep that promise.

Happiness surrounded me that day and I prayed and talked to God the whole day at work. *God, Thank You so much! You have always been there for me, when the storm clouds were always lurking around, hovering. You helped me through it all!*

I was the happiest person. I told my friends, they were so happy for me! They hugged my neck, and they all wanted to know what happened. My job hadn't made life easy over the last couple of months. Around the slow part of the year, January, February, March they cut hours. What David brought in didn't cover everything and we were barely surviving. I almost lost my home.

For weeks I couldn't sleep. I tossed and turned, worried and fretted. My stomach would hurt. My nerves were on the edge. But that was all over. I was on my way to recovery.

I received a phone call from Danna Hughes, President over Vietnam Wives, to congratulate me. It was really nice of her.

She said, "You winning your case will open the doors for other Vietnam Vets and widows, like yourself, they will hopefully win their cases."

"I hope so." I was very proud.

"Because you see it's not on the presumptive list you won, benefit of doubt, but that they admitted, didn't rule out, that the Glioblastoma *was* from exposure to Agent Orange in Vietnam."

I'd proven, with all of my hard work, paperwork, evidence and a great attorney, that Agent Orange killed my Tommy. My winning was all over the web, in newspapers, magazines etc.

I began to receive emails from other widows and Vietnam Vets thanking me and congratulating me for a job well done! It was awesome. I still get letters today, and that is one reason I decided to write this book.

After winning, I wondered what was stopping me from finishing what Tommy wanted to do all along. Why shouldn't I continue to help, support and encourage other Vets and their wives? It was what he would want and do if he were living.

I feel in my heart that spiritually, Tommy is still taking care of me! On another plane he's honored to be with God where there is no pain, no medicine problems, no worries, no bills only love.

On the following pages I have inserted the court documentation of winning my case.—Even though I did so much research, I have to give credit to that Bergmann and Moore, LLC for winning my DIC Widows Case. I hope something I've done, or maybe these documents, will guide other widows or widowers and veterans, that desperately need help, in the right direction. I keep them all in my heart, and in my prayers.

DEPARTMENT OF VETERANS AFFAIRS
Board of Veterans' Appeals
Washington DC 20420

JAN 2 6 2011

In Reply Refer To: (0141 A1)
25661338C

SHEREE E EVANS
1504 W. DANIELS
OZARK, MO 65721

Dear Appellant:

The Board of Veterans' Appeals has made a decision in this case, and a copy is enclosed. The records are being returned to the Department of Veterans Affairs office having jurisdiction over this matter.

Sincerely yours,

Robert C. Scharnberger
Acting Director
Office of Management, Planning and Analysis

Enclosures (1)

cc: JOSEPH MOORE
Bergmann & Moore, LLC
7920 Norfolk Avenue, Suite 700
Bethesda, MD 20814

BOARD OF VETERANS' APPEALS
DEPARTMENT OF VETERANS AFFAIRS
WASHINGTON, DC 20420

IN THE APPEAL OF
    SHEREE E. EVANS

XC 25 661 338

IN THE CASE OF
    EDWARD T. EVANS

DOCKET NO. 05-00 201   )   DATE JAN 2 6 2011

)

)

On appeal from the
Department of Veterans Affairs Regional Office in St. Louis, Missouri

THE ISSUE

Entitlement to service connection for the cause of the Veteran's death.

REPRESENTATION

Appellant represented by: Joseph R. Moore, Attorney-at-Law

WITNESS AT HEARING ON APPEAL

Appellant

IN THE APPEAL OF   XC 25 661 338
    SHEREE E. EVANS

IN THE CASE OF
    EDWARD T. EVANS

affirmative evidence to establish that the disease is due to an intercurrent injury or disease. 38 U.S.C. § 1116(a); 38 C.F.R. §§ 3.307(a)(6), 3.307(d)(1), 3.309(e). A veteran who served in the Republic of Vietnam during the Vietnam era shall be presumed to have been exposed during such service to an herbicide agent, unless there is affirmative evidence to establish that the veteran was not exposed to any such agent during that service. 38 U.S.C. § 1116(f).

Diseases associated with such exposure include: AL amyloidosis; chloracne or other acneform diseases consistent with chloracne; Type 2 diabetes (also known as Type II diabetes mellitus or adult-onset diabetes); Hodgkin's disease; ischemic heart disease (including, but not limited to, acute, subacute, and old myocardial infarction; atherosclerotic cardiovascular disease including coronary artery disease (including coronary spasm) and coronary bypass surgery; and stable, unstable and Prinzmetal's angina); all chronic B-cell leukemias (including, but not limited to, hairy-cell leukemia and chronic lymphocytic leukemia); multiple myeloma; non-Hodgkin's lymphoma; Parkinson's disease; acute and subacute peripheral neuropathy; porphyria cutanea tarda; prostate cancer; respiratory cancers (cancer of the lung, bronchus, larynx, or trachea); and soft-tissue sarcomas (other than osteosarcoma, chondrosarcoma, Kaposi's sarcoma, or mesothelioma). 38 C.F.R. § 3.309(e) Note 1; 75 Fed. Reg. 53,202 (August 31, 2010). For purposes of this section, the term ischemic heart disease does not include hypertension or peripheral manifestations of arteriosclerosis such as peripheral vascular disease or stroke, or any other condition that does not qualify within the generally accepted medical definition of Ischemic heart disease. 75 Fed. Reg. 53,202 (August 31, 2010) (to be codified as Note 3 in 38 C.F.R. § 3.309(e)). The Secretary of VA has determined that there is no positive association between exposure to herbicides and any other condition for which the Secretary has not specifically determined that a presumption of service connection is warranted. *See* Notice, 59 Fed. Reg. 341-346 (1994). *See also* 61 Fed. Reg. 41,442, 41,449 and 57,586, 57,589 (1996). A list of specific conditions not having a positive association was recently published by the Secretary. *See* Notice, 75 Fed. Reg. 81,332 (December 27, 2010).

SHEREE EVANS

IN THE APPEAL OF
   SHEREE E. EVANS

XC 25 661 338

IN THE CASE OF
   EDWARD T. EVANS

For presumptive service connection to be warranted, the herbicide-related disease shall have become manifest to a degree of 10 percent or more at any time after service, except that chloracne or other acneform disease consistent with chloracne, porphyria cutanea tarda, and acute and subacute peripheral neuropathy shall have become manifest to a degree of 10 percent or more within a year, and respiratory cancers within 30 years, after the last date on which the veteran was exposed to an herbicide agent during active military, naval, or air service. 38 C.F.R. § 3.307(a)(6)(ii). The last date on which such a veteran shall be presumed to have been exposed to an herbicide agent shall be the last date on which he or she served in the Republic of Vietnam during the Vietnam era. "Service in the Republic of Vietnam" includes service in the waters offshore and service in other locations if the conditions of service involved duty or visitation in the Republic of Vietnam. 38 C.F.R. § 3.307(a)(6)(iii). VA General Counsel has determined that the regulatory definition of "service in the Republic of Vietnam" in 38 C.F.R. § 3.307(a)(6)(iii), requires that an individual actually have been present within the boundaries of the Republic of Vietnam to be considered to have served there, through inclusion of the requirement for duty or visitation in the Republic of Vietnam. VAOPGCPREC 27-97.

In the present case, although the Veteran served in Vietnam and is entitled to the presumption of exposure to herbicides pursuant to 38 C.F.R. § 3.307(a)(6)(ii), the Board finds that presumptive service connection is not warranted for the cause of the Veteran's death because VA has not recognized cancers of the brain and nervous system (such as the Veteran's glioblastoma) as having a positive association with exposure to herbicides. Service connection may still be granted, however, if there is adequate evidence to establish that the etiology of the Veteran's glioblastoma was herbicide exposure in the Republic of Vietnam.

Of record are VA and private medical records from December 2002 through March 2003, which show how the diagnosis of glioblastoma was arrived at and includes

IN THE APPEAL OF   XC 25 661 338
   SHEREE E. EVANS

IN THE CASE OF
   EDWARD T. EVANS

the terminal records from the Community Hospice of Northeast Florida. These treatment records do not provide any opinion as to the possible etiology of the Veteran's glioblastoma.

The appellant has tried to establish an etiology by her own statements and with internet articles. As a lay person, however, she is not competent to establish a medical etiology merely by her own assertions because such matters require medical expertise. *See* 38 C.F.R. § 3.159(a)(1) (Competent medical evidence means evidence provided by a person who is qualified through education, training or experience to offer medical diagnoses, statements or opinions); *see also Espiritu v. Derwinski*, 2 Vet. App. 492, 494-95 (1992). Competency must be distinguished from weight and credibility, which are factual determinations going to the probative value of the evidence. *Rucker v. Brown*, 10 Vet. App. 67 (1997). Because the appellant is not professionally qualified to suggest a possible medical etiology, her statements are afforded little weight as to whether a nexus exists between the Veteran's glioblastoma and his presumed exposure to herbicides while serving in the Republic of Vietnam.

As to the internet articles the appellant submitted, a medical article or treatise "can provide important support when combined with an opinion of a medical professional" if the medical article or treatise evidence discusses generic relationships with a degree of certainty such that, under the facts of a specific case, there is at least "plausible causality" based upon objective facts rather than on an unsubstantiated lay medical opinion. *Mattern v. West*, 12 Vet. App. 222, 228 (1999).; *see also Sacks v. West*, 11 Vet. App. 314 (1998); *Wallin v. West*, 11 Vet. App. 509 (1998). The articles submitted by the appellant were not accompanied by the opinion of any medical expert linking the Veteran's glioblastoma to his in-service exposure to herbicides. Thus, the medical articles submitted are insufficient to establish the required medical nexus.

SHEREE EVANS

IN THE APPEAL OF
    SHEREE E. EVANS

XC 25 661 338

IN THE CASE OF
    EDWARD T. EVANS

However, several medical opinions are of record relating to this question. A VHA medical opinion was obtained in November 2008 in which a VA physician stated that "[a]s glioblastoma multiforme is not on the VA's Agent Orange List of presumptive disabilities ... then the answer is: [n]o I cannot with any acceptable degree of medical certainty and without resort to speculation – that (sic) there is any basis for the inclusion of 'Agent orange exposure' as either a principle or a contributory cause of death." Based upon this medical opinion, the Board issued a decision in February 2009 denying the appellant's claim. The appellant appealed that denial to the Court of Appeals for Veterans Claims (Court). Pursuant to a Joint Motion for Remand, in November 2009 the Court vacated the February 2009 Board decision and remanded the appellant's appeal. In the Joint Motion for Remand, the parties agreed that the Board had erred in relying on the November 2008 VHA medical opinion as it was inadequate because the sole basis for the VHA examiner's opinion that there was no relationship between Agent Orange exposure and glioblastoma multiforme was that it was not on the presumptive list of cancers. As a consequence of the Joint Motion for Remand, therefore, this VHA medical opinion is inadequate and cannot be utilized in deciding the appellant's case at this time.

The appellant's appeal was returned to the Board and, in June 2010, another VHA opinion was requested. In making the request, the Board noted that the appellant has also claimed that the Veteran's glioblastoma may also have been caused by exposure to DDT and/or Dapsone, that the Veteran's glioblastoma was a metastasized cancer from the Veteran's previous testicular cancer, and that the Veteran's cancer was not glioblastoma but another form of cancer for which VA has recognized an association with exposure to herbicides. Consequently, the Board requested that the VHA medical expert (an oncologist preferably with knowledge on diseases associated with herbicide and other chemical exposure) to answer the following questions after reviewing the claims file:

IN THE APPEAL OF   XC 25 661 338
  SHEREE E. EVANS

IN THE CASE OF
  EDWARD T. EVANS

1. Is glioblastoma multiforme the appropriate diagnosis of the brain tumor that is listed on the death certificate as the primary cause of the Veteran's death? Please answer yes or no and explain your answer referring to all supporting evidence.

2. Is it at least as likely as not (i.e., at least a 50 percent probability) that the primary cause of the Veteran's death (i.e. glioblastoma multiforme) is proximately due to or the result of one of the following: (1) exposure to herbicides (e.g., Agent Orange) in the Republic of Vietnam; (2) the Veteran's intake of Dapsone tablets in service; or (3) exposure to DDT in the Republic of Vietnam?

3. Was the glioblastoma multiforme a primary cancer or a metastasized cancer from the Veteran's prior testicular cancer? If it was a metastasized cancer, is it at least as likely as not that the testicular cancer the Veteran had in 1995 was proximately due to or the result of one of the following: (1) exposure to herbicides (e.g., Agent Orange) in the Republic of Vietnam; (2) the Veteran's intake of Dapsone tablets in service; or (3) exposure to DDT in the Republic of Vietnam?

4. Is it at least as likely as not that the Veteran's testicular cancer contributed materially and significantly to his death, that it combined to cause death; or that it aided or lent assistance to the production of death?

The requested VHA medical opinion was received in September 2010. The following were the medical expert's responses to the above questions:

1. Yes, the patient was diagnosed with glioblastoma multiforme which is a pathological diagnosis made by a biopsy. This diagnosis carries a poor prognosis and led to the patient's placement in hospice care and ultimate demise.

IN THE APPEAL OF   XC 25 661 338
   SHEREE E. EVANS

IN THE CASE OF
   EDWARD T. EVANS

2. No, I do not find any current scientific evidence in the medical literature of an association between glioblastoma multiforme and any of the above mentioned circumstances.

3. The glioblastoma multiforme was a primary cancer.

4. No. The patient's testicular cancer does not appear to have contributed to his death.

Essentially, the VHA medical expert's opinion was that the Veteran's death was caused by the glioblastoma and it was not as likely as not that the glioblastoma was proximately due to or the result of exposure to herbicides (e.g., Agent Orange) in the Republic of Vietnam; the Veteran's intake of Dapsone tablets in service; or exposure to DDT in the Republic of Vietnam; moreover, the Veteran's prior testicular cancer was not a contributory cause of the Veteran's death.

The appellant was provided a copy of this medical opinion in October 2010. In response, the appellant via her attorney submitted a medical statement from a private physician dated in November 2010. This physician stated that he reviewed the medical records made available to him and that it is clear the Veteran died as a result of glioblastoma multiforme (GBM). He stated that "GBM is a highly aggressive form of brain cancer which, when left untreated, unusually results in death in less than three months. Established brain tumor risk factors (exposure to ionizing radiation, rare mutations of penetrant genes, and familial history) explain only a small proportion of brain tumors. Genetic and environmental characteristics likely play a role in familial aggregation of GBM." (Footnote omitted.) The physician notes that the Veteran's history is notable for active service in Vietnam and presumed exposure to Agent Orange and 2, 3, 7, 8-tetrachlorodibenzo-ρ-dioxin (TCDD) a common contaminant. Citing to multiple sources, the physician stated that "[m]uch research has been done to find a link between the increasing prevalence of brain cancers and environmental exposures. In 2001, Zhen, et. al. concluded that subjects who worked in plumbing, heating, and air conditioning;

IN THE APPEAL OF   XC 25 661 338
      SHEREE E. EVANS

IN THE CASE OF
      EDWARD T. EVANS

electrical services; gasoline service stations; and *military occupations* experienced a significantly increased risk. Many other studies have found similar relationships between brain cancers and herbicide exposure through farming or the agricultural industry. TCDD has also been shown to cause cancer in laboratory animals at a variety of sites. If TCDD has similar effects on cell regulation in humans, it is plausible that it could have an effect on human cancer incidence as well. More recent research is focusing on the role of dioxin specific receptor activation and subsequent signal transduction pathways which lead to carcinogenesis and glioblastoma formation. To be fair, much of this medical evidence is very recent, but it appears neither the 2008 nor the 2010 VA opinions reviewed or cited any of this growing body of evidence for a nexus between Agent Orange exposure and GBM tumorigenesis." (Footnotes omitted.)

This physician further stated that he reviewed the Veteran's treatment history and also carefully reviewed the VA medical opinions in this case. He stated that "[c]urrent research suggests that there is a causal relationship between herbicide exposure and the development of GBM. Particularly given that [the Veteran] experienced no other major risk factors for the development of GBM, aside from the environmental exposure to Agent Orange, it is my medical opinion that it is more likely than not that the glioblastoma of the brain that caused [the Veteran's] death was a result of his in-service Agent Orange exposure. I base this opinion on my review of [the Veteran's] military and medical history as well as my review of the current medical literature on the topic. I concur with the Medical Examiner and agree that Agent Orange exposure was a contributing factor in [the Veteran's] death." It is noted that this physician cited to 11 sources in support of his medical opinion.

After considering both of the medical opinions obtained, on their face, the Board cannot conclude that either medical opinion is not factually accurate, fully articulated, and with sound reasoning for the conclusion arrived at. Consequently, both medical opinions are equally probative. *See Nieves-Rodriguez v. Peake*, 22

IN THE APPEAL OF   XC 25 661 338
    SHEREE E. EVANS

IN THE CASE OF
    EDWARD T. EVANS

Vet. App. 295 (2008). Thus, the evidence as to an etiologic relationship between the Veteran's glioblastoma and his presumed exposure to herbicides while serving in the Republic of Vietnam appears to be in equipoise.

The Board also notes that, in June 2010, the VA published the May 2008 Update from the National Academy of Science (NAS). *See* 75 Fed. Reg. 32,540-53 (June 8, 2010). In the May 2008 Update, with regard to brain cancer, the NAS concluded that the categorization in prior updates (limited or suggestive evidence of no association) should be revised to inadequate or insufficient to determine whether there is an association between herbicide exposure and brain cancer and other nervous system cancers on the basis of detailed evaluation of the epidemiologic evidence from new and previously reported studies of populations with potential herbicide exposure. *Id.* at p. 32,546. Essentially the NAS upgraded the categorization of brain cancer causing the question of whether there is a link between brain cancer and herbicide exposure to be more uncertain and opening the door for medical opinions on the issue of etiology.

The Board must assess the credibility and weight of all the evidence, including the medical evidence, to determine its probative value, accounting for evidence that it finds to be persuasive or unpersuasive, and providing reasons for rejecting any evidence favorable to the claimant. Equal weight is not accorded to each piece of evidence contained in the record; every item of evidence does not have the same probative value. Nevertheless, when, after considering all the evidence, a reasonable doubt arises regarding a determinative issue, the benefit of the doubt shall be given to the claimant. 38 U.S.C.A. § 5107; 38 C.F.R. § 3.102.

The medical opinions being of equal probative value, the Board finds that the evidence is in equipoise as to whether the etiology of the Veteran's glioblastoma that caused his death was his presumed exposure to herbicides while serving in the Republic of Vietnam. The evidence being in equipoise, the benefit of the doubt is

IN THE APPEAL OF   XC 25 661 338
   SHEREE E. EVANS

IN THE CASE OF
   EDWARD T. EVANS

given to the appellant. Consequently, the Board concludes that service connection for the cause of the Veteran's death (i.e., glioblastoma) is warranted.

ORDER

Entitlement to service connection for the cause of the Veteran's death is granted.

_____
John E. Ormond, Jr.
Veterans Law Judge, Board of Veterans' Appeals

My Surprise Birthday Present

Miracles of Joy!

After the news spread over our country that I had won, I received a phone call from Mike Landis with KY3TV in Springfield, Missouri. He wanted to interview me on winning my DIC Widows Pension. Our conversation went something like this.

Mike said, "I'll make arrangements to come to your home if you agree."

I thought for a minute then answered. "Better yet, how about going to Missouri veterans Cemetery off of Evans Road? Tommy is buried in the wall there."

"What a great idea!"

"Great!" My heart was happy that he'd liked my suggestion, so we made arrangements for the day, and time.

The day came and as I got ready, I realized something. It was my birthday! I couldn't believe I hadn't thought of it the day we made the arrangements, but I was thinking more about being on television and getting my story out there. Of all days, Mike had chosen my birthday. What a special gift he was giving me. My birthday was complete!

Tommy would have been proud. He had always done something special for me on that day! This must have been another sign from heaven. Tommy had arranged this birthday surprise.

In my mind there was one more heavenly sign that day. It was cloudy and cold when I arrived at the cemetery. Mike and his camera man were pulling equipment out of their vehicle and asked where they needed to set up.

I went over and stood where my Tommy is in the wall. They finished getting ready and we started the interview and I shivered in the gloomy, overcast chilled air. Then something amazing happened. As soon as I began to answer Mike's first question, the clouds parted and rays of sunshine beamed down on us. The warmth came over me, and I realized God was clearing the clouds so Tommy could see what was taking place. I felt tears well in my eyes, but they subsided when Mike continued with his questions. Apparently I was the only one who noticed the change, but that's okay, it was my special birthday gift from God.

I told him my moto: Fight to Make It Right! And never give up!

After, the interview someone in charge of cemetery came over to us and asked who gave us permission to be there? I told him "This is a Missouri Veterans Cemetery and it's open to the public. My husband, proud USMC Vietnam Veteran, Edward T. Evans is inside this wall."

His attitude changed. "Well, if I'd have known, I would have made sure the place was looking its best."

That made me mad. I looked him straight in the eye. "Shouldn't it be taken care of all the time, not just because we had a camera here?"

He had no reply so I walked away from him. I followed Mike to their van and decided I wasn't going to let the likes of that cemetery guy ruin my special day.

"Mike?" I said.

"Yes, ma'am?"

"I just want you to know you gave me one of the best birthday presents I've ever had."

He looked at me with surprise in his eyes. "Is this your birthday?"

I smiled. "Yes!"

"I didn't know that. Happy Birthday!"

I laughed out loud. "Happy Birthday indeed. God is everywhere and my Tommy now has angel wings." I stepped forward and hugged the journalist. "Thank you!"

Below is an article that was on KY3 the day before the interview. After that is the interview.

Widow from Ozark wins VA benefits for husband's brain cancer from Agent Orange in Vietnam

February 17, 2011|by KY3 News |

OZARK, Mo. -- A woman whose husband died eight years ago from brain cancer has won an appeal at the U.S. Veterans Administration. Sheree Evans claimed his death resulted from Edward Evans' exposure to Agent Orange when he was a Marine in the Vietnam War. A law firm in the Washington, D.C., area says the ruling means Evans will receive widow's benefits from the Department of Veterans Affairs.

The law firm, Bergmann & Moore, says the ruling is the first time that the VA has admitted a link between Agent Orange exposure and glioblastoma multiform, the brain cancer that killed Edward Evans in 2003. It says the ruling on Jan. 26 by the Court of Appeals for Veterans Appeals could mean other Vietnam War veterans with brain cancer and their survivors could also win VA benefits.

Agent Orange is a chemical that U.S. military officials used to kill foliage in the jungles of Vietnam to try to make it more difficult for North Vietnamese and Viet Cong soldiers to hide from and ambush U.S. and South Vietnamese soldiers and Marines. Studies link exposure to dioxin TCDD, an ingredient in Agent Orange, to cancers in laboratory animals. Because of the studies and other human ailments linked to the chemical, Agent Orange is no longer used.

Widow wins legal battle in husband's death linked to 'Agent Orange'
Agent Orange was used during Vietnam War as an herbicide, has since been linked to cancer
February 18, 2011|by Mike Landis, KY3 News |

OZARK, Mo. - It's now been eight long years since Sheree Evans lost the love of her life.

Her husband, Edward Tommy Evans, had lost his fight with cancer.

"We related to each other, Sheree said. "He laughed a lot. He made people laugh."

But the battle for Tommy, a decorated former Marine, was long from over.

Before his passing, Tommy came to believe his brain cancer resulted from his exposure to a deadly toxin while serving in the Vietnam War in the late 1960s.

That chemical, Agent Orange, was used by the U.S. military during the Vietnam War to destroy foliage in the jungles. The goal was to strip enemy soldiers of a place to hide-out.

Experts say at least 20-million gallons of the herbicide were sprayed between 1962 and 1971.

Thought of as harmless at the time, Agent Orange would eventually be linked to at least 40 different types of illnesses and cancers. Thousands of Vietnam vets are believed to have fallen sick in recent years due to the chemical.

"It was just horrendous they were just trying to keep each other alive, being fired at. They weren't even thinking about chemically getting sprayed," Sheree said.

The Veterans Administration recognizes dozens of sicknesses and disabilities linked to Agent Orange. However, the VA said it could find no link between the chemical and the type of brain cancer Tommy had (Glioblastoma Multiform).

That decision meant his sickness wasn't classified as war-related, and Sheree wouldn't qualify for survivor's benefits upon her husband's death.

"I know that he cried a lot and wrote me a love letter he was very disappointed. But I promised him and that gave him hope," remembered Sheree.

She kept her promise once Tommy died. It was a fight that would take her case to top Veterans Administration leaders. Then, on January 26th, she won an appeal of her claim's denial.

Sheree's law firm, Bergmann & Moore, LLC, stated the VA admitted a possible link between Agent Orange and Glioblastoma Multiform (GM). The ruling stated there was equal amount of medical evidence in favor and against a connection.

The VA has yet to add GM to its presumptive list of recognized side-effects of Agent Orange. However, the recent ruling could lead to the illness being included. The list has grown several times over the years as new sicknesses manifested themselves in affected veterans.

Sheree hopes her victory will help other families involved in similar cases with the VA and Agent Orange.

She's making plans to write a book detailing her and Tommy's story.

My Tribute of Appreciation

Thank You for Bringing Awareness to Others

Tim King

Tim's years as a Human Rights reporter have taken on many dimensions; he has rallied for a long list of cultures and populations and continues to every day, with a strong and direct concentration on the 2009 Genocide of Tamil Hindus and Christians in Sri Lanka. As a result of his long list of reports exposing war crimes against Tamil people, Tim was invited to be the keynote speaker at the FeTNA (Federation of Tamil Sangams of North America) Conference in Baltimore, in July 2012. This is the largest annual gathering of North American Tamils; Tim addressed more than 3000 people and was presented with a traditional Sri Lanka 'blessed garland' and a shawl as per the tradition and custom of Tamil Nadu

Tim's Background prior to Salem-News.com

Tim`s history is steeped in his ability and desire to tell a great story - which first led him to the television newsroom in 1988, serving as News Anchor/Reporter for Lincoln City, Oregon`s cable TV station, TV 10. That`s where Tim found his calling.

Tim King in Afghanistan

Since those first years, Tim has moved on to serve as News Photojournalist/Reporter for KATU (ABC), Photojournalist at KVVU (FOX), KVBC (NBC), and KYMA (NBC), the News Assignment Editor for KVVU (FOX) in Las Vegas, NV, as well as radio News Director (KBCH/KCRF). In addition, he was the Producer/Host for the `Coast Entertainment Show`, Executive Producer (creator) of the TV series `Hot Wheels in Las Vegas`, and Executive Producer of the 30-minute documentary `Fallen Fortress at Cape Lookout` which aired on Oregon Public Broadcasting in 1993.

Also significant among his achievements are the 2 years he spent as a Wildlife Rescue team leader on the coast of Oregon; and his service in the US Marine Corps with MWSG-37 in the 3rd Marine Air Wing at El Toro.

Tim`s career in the broadcast industry has afforded him many opportunities to cover incredible stories as well as meet innumerable celebrities and dignitaries. He has flown in many military planes including an F-16 Air Force Fighter, and produced a three-part series on aviation history of the Southwest region of the United States. Aviation is one of Tim`s passions.

Tim majored in journalism at Cuesta College in San Luis Obispo, California. He holds numerous awards for reporting, photography, writing and editing, including the Oregon AP Award for Spot News Photographer of the Year (2004), the first place Electronic Media Award in Spot News, Las Vegas, (1998), Oregon AP Cooperation Award (1991); and several other awards including the 2005 Red Cross Good Neighborhood Award for reporting.

I know that God puts people in places at the time He feel you need to cross paths. The first time I ever hear of Tim Andrew King was when he contacted me and told me he had written an article about me winning my case. I was pleased that Tim was a Marine Veteran the same as Tommy.

The story he wrote is amazing. I couldn't help but read it over and over. It captured my whole being and I realized I really did make a difference. I had, and hopefully will continue to, help others that are fighting the same issues I did, win their case.

Feb-18-2011 23:58

Wounded by the North Vietnamese, Killed by Monsanto

Tim King Salem-News.com

Agent Orange, Vietnam, and the Struggle No American Should Ever Know. Semper fi Edward Evans...

(SALEM, Ore.) - Edward Evans passed away from brain cancer, *Glioblastoma Multiforme* (GM) in March of 2003. His wife Sheree has been fighting for widow's benefits from the Department of Veterans Affairs (VA) for her husband's cause of death as a result of Agent Orange exposure in the ensuing years.

As a Marine in Vietnam, Edward Evans was awarded the Purple Heart for wounds suffered in combat. The wounds that killed him were inflicted by American politics and a company called **Monsanto**.

Marines like Edward Evans were sometimes frequently exposed to the deadly chemical Agent Orange in the Vietnam War, but the government and the deadly chemical's manufacturer **Monsanto** have fought tooth and nail to avoid responsibility or accountability.

Even when the occasional politician tries to help veterans, others throw roadblocks in the way; blocking funding and support.

While there have been breakthroughs in this fight for transparency and simple honesty regarding Agent Orange, the particular condition that Ed suffered from turned out to be one of the most challenging obstacles for Sheree.

She had to show that his exposure to Agent Orange caused the development of brain cancer.

Sheree and Edward Evans

The Veterans Administration had consistently maintained that brain cancer is not on their list of Agent Orange-related disabilities, and, as a result, that there is no medical link for the development of this specific cancer to Agent Orange Exposure.

In her article published last December by Salem-News.com, *Dioxin and Glioblastoma in the Vietnam Veteran Population*, Eileen Whitacre described how *the tracking of glioblastomas in the aging population of Vietnam veterans exposed to dioxin has been neglected. The poorly researched and nonsensical U.S. AIR FORCE RANCH HAND study has been sighted as evidence. The Seveso Italy incident is also used as evidence.*

US plane loaded with Agent Orange prior to a mission over Vietnam.

The TEN YEAR MORTALITY STUDY OF THE POPULATION INVOLVED IN THE SEVSO INCIDENT IN 1976 reported by the **American Journal of Epidemiology Vol. 129 No.6** *states "a significant increased relative risks were noted for peritoneum, pleura, melanoma and brain cancer in the first study period."*

The significant report by Admiral Zumwalt Jr. has been squashed...[1]

So once again, it is as simple as the fact that the government and its crime partner **Monsanto** have no adherence to honesty whatsoever.

Read: Monsanto is the Real Food Terror Threat by Chris Hinyub

They have damned well known that there is a serious detectable connection between brain cancer and Agent Orange.

It was a real honor to publish **VA Links Brain Cancer to Agent Orange Exposure in Recent Court Decision** this week, and today learning that this Marine's name was added to the *The Agent Orange Quilt of Tears* made my heart soar.

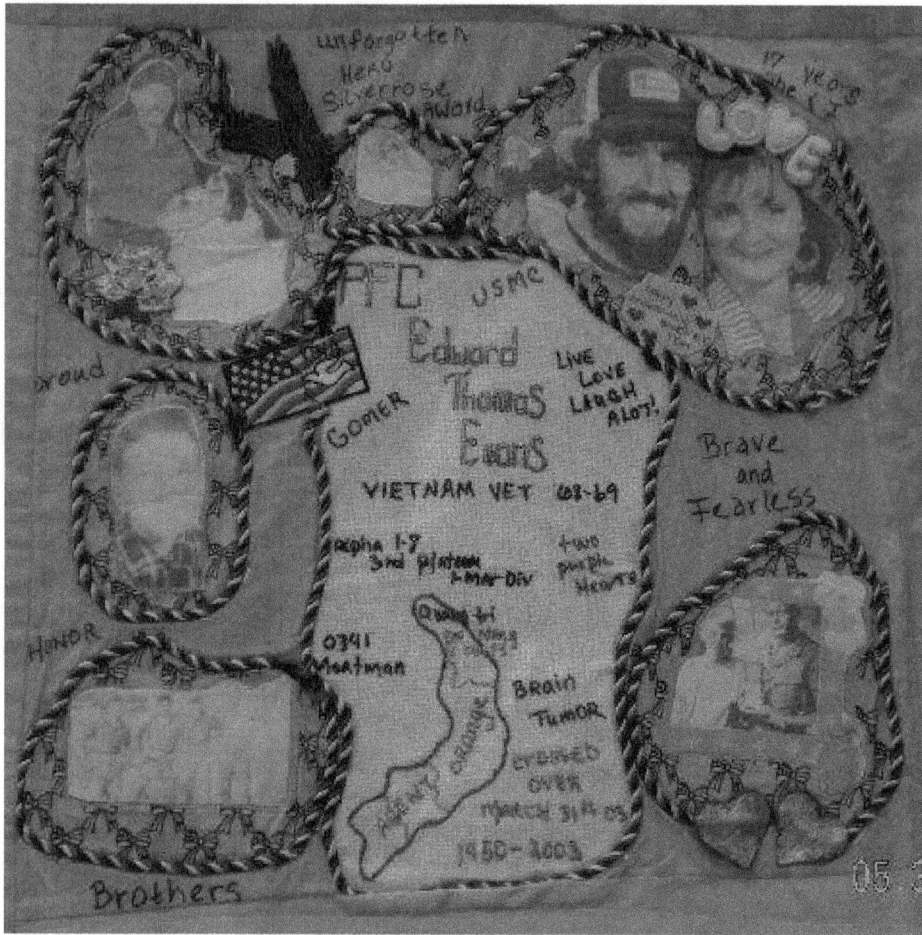

Visit the: *Agent Orange Quilt of Tears*

The article was a news release from the attorney representing Sheree Evans, widow of Vietnam Marine veteran Edward Evans.[2]

She made the quilt block for her late husband several years ago, just after Edward passed away. It has been a part of the *Agent Orange Quilt Of Tears* since early 2004. His block is on Quilt #16.

The Honor Roll can be seen at the link in this paragraph. Sheree & Edward Evans' story is a very familiar one to those who keep up on the politics of Agent Orange.[3].

We always hear about the way veterans were treated by anti-war people during the Vietnam years. The people who wanted others to stop *dying* in a war the US had no apparent real interest in winning, are historically held out to dry for "costing" the US the war.

Be it the war's journalists who told the truth of what was taking place, or those who took the time to speak out against it; the right wing actually 'blames' the loss of the Vietnam War on the exposure of the truth, and that is not true.

There was more than one point where the US could have brought the North Vietnamese to their knees but American politicians lacked the political will to win, and *that* is the truth.

While the civilian populace was unkind to the Vietnam veteran in many respects, much of the talk about anti-war demonstrators spitting on returning veterans was propaganda also[4].

What we seldom hear about is the really ugly side of the story; the part about how people returning from the war in Vietnam were not well regarded by 'The Greatest Generation' - WWII veterans, at least not in the early years.

Few people understood what these veterans had faced in Vietnam. It actually took Sylvester Stallone's role in 'Rambo' to cause the average American to understand what the fighting men of the Vietnam War had attempted to survive.

But that did indeed work, and people younger and older than the Vietnam Generation suddenly had something to gauge the Vietnam veteran's experience against, and this included the WWII people who were about the age of the average Vietnam veteran today; around 60.

The 'Greatest Generation' won the Second World War, but they also dropped two atomic bombs, built internment camps for Japanese-Americans on the west coast, and they kept Blacks segregated in the Armed Forces until 1947.

Equally sinister, this generation also filled the business suits at **Monsanto** in the 1960's.

Map of Vietnam and surrounding SE Asian countries today.

These *people* were responsible for the deadly reckless business practices that led to Agent Orange, a 'chemical defoliant' - being sprayed over Vietnam's jungles to kill the vegetation that hid enemy forces.

They sure deserve the **'effectiveness'** award; **Monsanto** has led to more suffering and pain and birth defects and early deaths than any company in history. Nobody has killed more people than **Monsanto**[5].

It breaks my heart to consider what the Vietnam Generation had to go through; apparently WWII really gave America confidence that it held the white knight's role in the world and ridding Europe of the Nazi presence was an honorable pursuit.

The Vietnam veteran was not even allowed to join the **Veterans of Foreign Wars** in the early years. That regard certainly didn't help the Vietnam vet find justice in the world of big business and politics.

Kathy Lee was a first Lieutenant in the US Army during the Vietnam War. She served in the Nurse Corps which had a very directed job of saving people' lives. "I wasn't really welcome in the VFW. It was a good old boys club, and the WWII veterans did not really recognize the Vietnam veterans and they did not accept women."[6].

Women, nurses; who have served in dangerous combat conditions since the beginning of time, were not allowed into the Veteran of Foreign Wars simply because they were women. Not what I'd call a *generational* accomplishment. I know from covering the war in Iraq and Afghanistan that US nurses treat *everyone*; they don't discriminate and locals, even suspected 'insurgents', are medically well cared for. Our writer Dr. Leveque, who fought in WWII and then treated Vietnam veterans for Post Traumatic Stress Disorder (PTSD), has written about how nurses are historically treated with indifference by the military and VA[8].

I will say though that these WWII guys who weathered time came to embrace and love people like Edward Evans; in some cases too late but not every time.

And here is the caveat of Edward Evans' generation; the second the first troops began rotating home from the terrible war in Iraq and Afghanistan, the Vietnam vets were there to welcome them home and they took the steps to ensure that these troops are well regarded and not trashed.

We apparently take a long time to learn, but it is the steadfastness of people like Ed Evans that created a welcome home platform for today's veteran, regardless of whether or not the war they fight in is popular or a huge national mistake.

The challenges Vietnam veterans were different in many ways. In addition to extreme drug abuse, one tragic example is suicide. According to the Vietnam veteran operated Website *capveterans.com*

"We lost almost 59,000 men and women during the 16 years of Viet Nam. As of 5 years after the war was officially over, we had 150,000 Viet Nam Vets that had committed suicide."[9]

The thing is that while many committed suicide, far more did not and still had to check out far ahead of schedule.

From the: **Wikipedia page on Monsanto**

The 1940s saw Monsanto become a leading manufacturer of plastics, including polystyrene, and synthetic fibers.

Since then, it has remained one of the top 10 US chemical companies. Other major products have included the herbicides 2,4,5-T, DDT, and Agent Orange used primarily during the Vietnam War as a defoliant agent (later found to be contaminated during manufacture with highly carcinogenic dioxin), the artificial sweetener aspartame (NutraSweet), bovine somatotropin (bovine growth hormone (BST)), and PCBs.

Also in this decade, Monsanto operated the Dayton Project, and later Mound Laboratories in Miamisburg, Ohio, for the Manhattan Project, the development of the first nuclear weapons and, after 1947, the Atomic Energy Commission[7].

Edward Evans as a young Marine during Vietnam War.

These war fighters had a fierce conflict on their hands in Vietnam. Veterans suffer and have not only suffered wounds from weapons like the AK-47, mortars, rockets or landmines, not even the nightmare and terrible memories; instead it is that chemical gift wrapped in the red, white and blue wrapper of America's business spirit, that killer Agent Orange that imperils our men *and* women. [10].

Agent Orange, a product of the company **Monsanto** that is a criminal group that should be forced to shut down all of its operation and liquidate its asset to the families of veteran and also to the Vietnamese who suffer horrible birth defects to this day[11].

Monsanto killed Edward Evan. He did everything right; he was an ideal American youth who chose to serve his country in the fullest extent by joining the United States Marine Corps. **Monsanto** killed my friend Bill Cheer also. His death from cancer came just after he found what it took to go back to SE Asia, in the early 1990's. He was so thrilled, everything looked so good for him, but the weight loss was startling. The funny thing is that he looked an awful lot like Edward Evan and they both did their best to survive that war. I think they both at one time thought they had, but in the end they did not. They were killed by a war in SE Asia by a weapon created and built in the land of sour apple pie[12].

Monsanto, headquartered in Creve Coeur, Missouri; has been a hazardous company for a long time, and today they are the group behind the mad scientist seeds, known as GMO- genetically modified seeds are Monsanto's baby. They are unnatural, they are wrong, and a scourge in this world. They are created by mutating nature.

If they aren't killing people with herbicides or atomic bombs, **Monsanto** is trying to steal your life at the dinner table. If and when Revolution takes off in America, it won't be a bunch of disgruntled racists with tea party signs, it will be real people and they will move toward Monsanto.

The latest salt rubbed in our wounds was not unexpected; it was a Monsanto official finding his way into a nice influential position with the Food and Drug Administration. It is in every respect, a result of moral bankruptcy[13].

Another non-friend to the Vietnam Veteran can be the fellow Vietnam Vet who turns politician. In Virginia you have people like Senator Jim Webb who had the chance to help those suffering from Agent Orange poisoning, and instead drove a knife in their backs, even as the head of the VA was pushing to help[14].

Those who turn their backs on their brothers and sisters deserve nothing less than the legacy they create. Those who help and do what they can can be remarkable; people like Sheree Evans. I admire and respect her so much, as I do her late husband. I wish I could have known him. There is a brotherhood aspect with Marine veterans that is far reaching. It

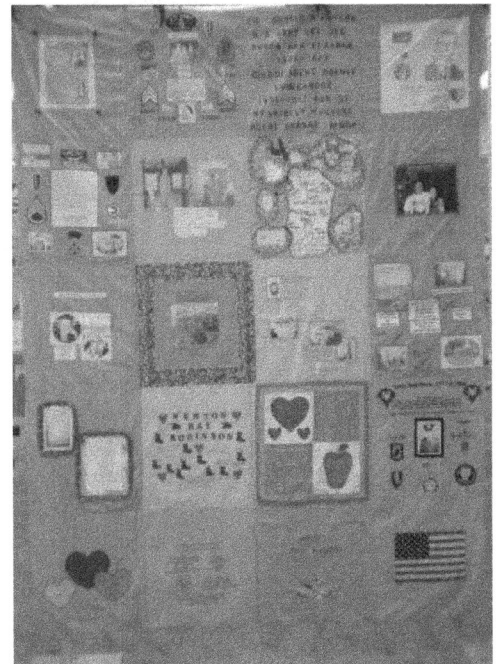
Agent Orange Quilt Of Tears

also includes every soldier, sailor, airman and civilian who served or worked in Vietnam during the war.

I hope news reporters and editors reading this can appreciate that Agent Orange and Monsanto are subjects needing a lot of attention. The Vietnam Generation is retiring and while I have had many friends in media who served in Vietnam; people like Paul Hanson who used to work at KATU Channel-2

News in Portland, my old station, and still is going strong at Public Radio Station KQED in northern California, there are not enough and it is up to the new generations to keep the awareness factor in front of people. Hundreds of thousands of American Vietnam vet children have been born with birth defects[15].

Monsanto and **Agent Orange** are gifts from your government that keep on giving, and if they ever pay a cent in return, it will never be enough.

Semper fi Edward Evans.

Salem-News.com has a long list of links to articles related to Agent Orange: Salem-News.com Agent Orange articles Page 1

Referenced sources:

[1] **Dioxin and Glioblastoma in the Vietnam Veteran Population - Eileen Whitacre Special to Salem-News.com**

[2] **VA Links Brain Cancer to Agent Orange Exposure in Recent Court Decision - Salem-News.com**

[3] **Agent Orange Quilt Of Tears**

[4] **Who really Spat on Veterans During the Vietnam War? - Tim King Salem-News.com**

[5] **Agent Orange: The Damage Lives On In Vietnam - Chuck Palazzo Salem-News.com**

[6] **Vietnam Veterans and the VFW - jointheelite.org**

[7] **Wikipedia page on Monsanto**

[8] **Military Nurses: VA's Shabby Treatment of Forgotten Angels - Dr. Phil Leveque Salem-News.com**

[9] **capveterans.com**

[10] **A Loss of Innocence: My Story - By Lesli Moore Dahlke - Special to Salem-News.com**

[11] **Victims of Victims - Chuck Palazzo Salem-News.com.**

[12] **While We Were Sleeping...GM Food and the Brink of No Return - April Scott Salem-News.com**

[13] **Monsanto Executive Appointed to High Level Position in the FDA - Marianne Skolek Salem-News.com.**

[14] **Turncoat Senator Jim Webb's Attempt to Take Down Shinseki Over Agent Orange Advocacy - Chuck Palazzo Salem-News.com**

[15] **Photograph of Danang Girl Affected by Agent Orange Wins UNICEF Photo of the Year Contest - Salem-News.com**

Tim has since become like a brother to me. I was very honored when he invited me to represent his mission *Operation Red Dragonfly*. I am currently ORD's contact coordinator

This is the t-shirt logo I designed for Operation Red Dragonfly. It covers all states, though th one shown is for Missouri.

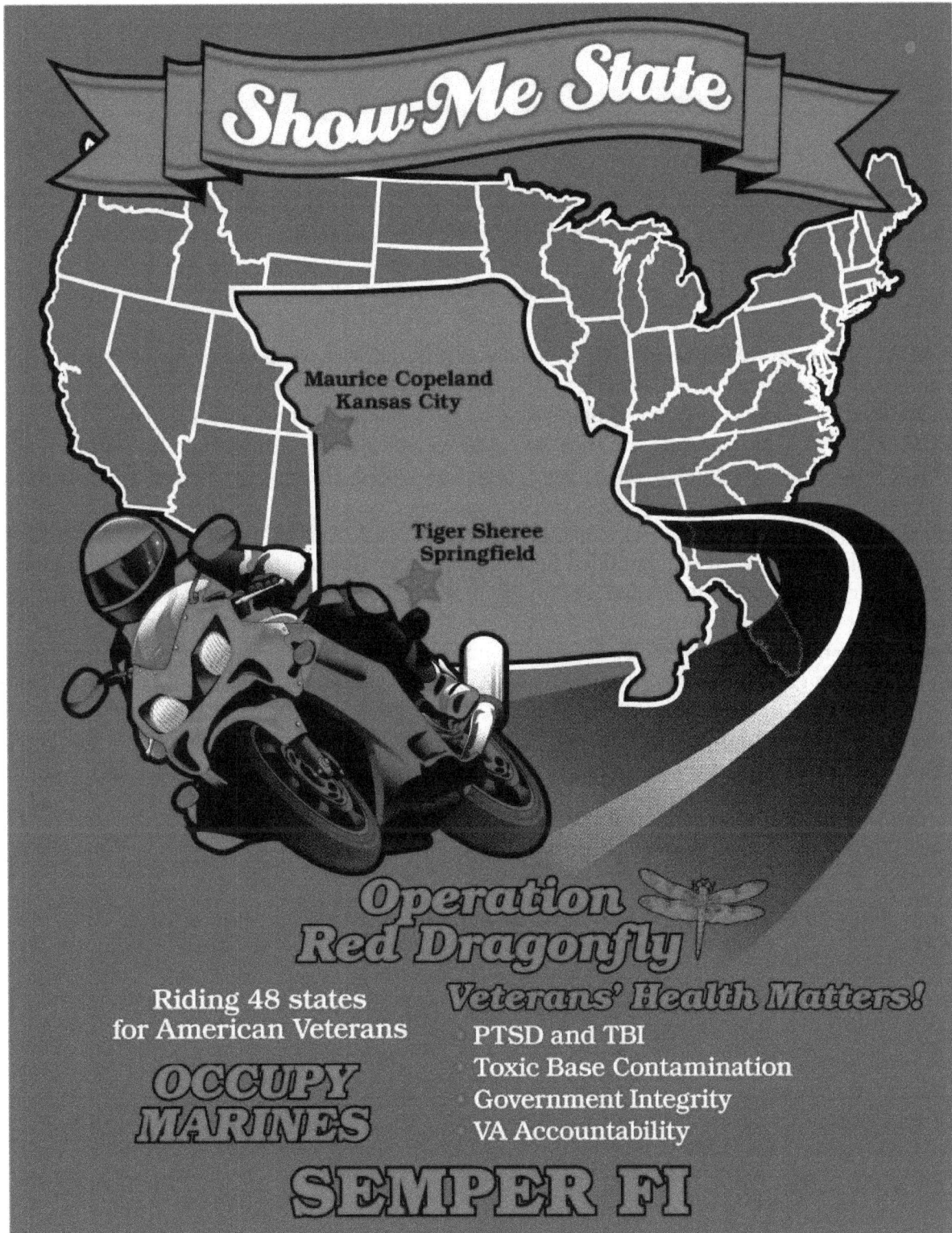

Operation Red Dragonfly

Paying it Forward

What is Operation Red Dragonfly? It's a teaching program that brings awareness to the public about many things. Tim journeys across America speaking out to the public about our military veterans, their healthcare issues, PTSD, TBI, Agent Orange, base contamination and motor cycle safety.

In 2013 Tim took his first ride. He rode solo and was faced with many obstacles—from weather to motorcycle mishaps—sometimes, funds were few. He would choose gas before food so he could continue on with his mission.

He slept in a sleeping bag at rest stops, or out at State parks but he didn't care. You see he wasn't doing this for himself, he was being pulled by a higher force. He wanted to help all his living brothers, sisters, military veterans that needed so much help. Still today he is propelled forward in this undertaking.

I think that it's truly remarkable. Think of yourself. Would you be able to endure such a feat of unbelievable courage and stamina? I myself would be the first one to say, I couldn't. But I can other ways.

I feel a rewarding sense of duty to my Tommy, and all military family. Now we are focused on Operation Red Dragonfly—2—2015, and Tim already has several venues lined up, across the country.

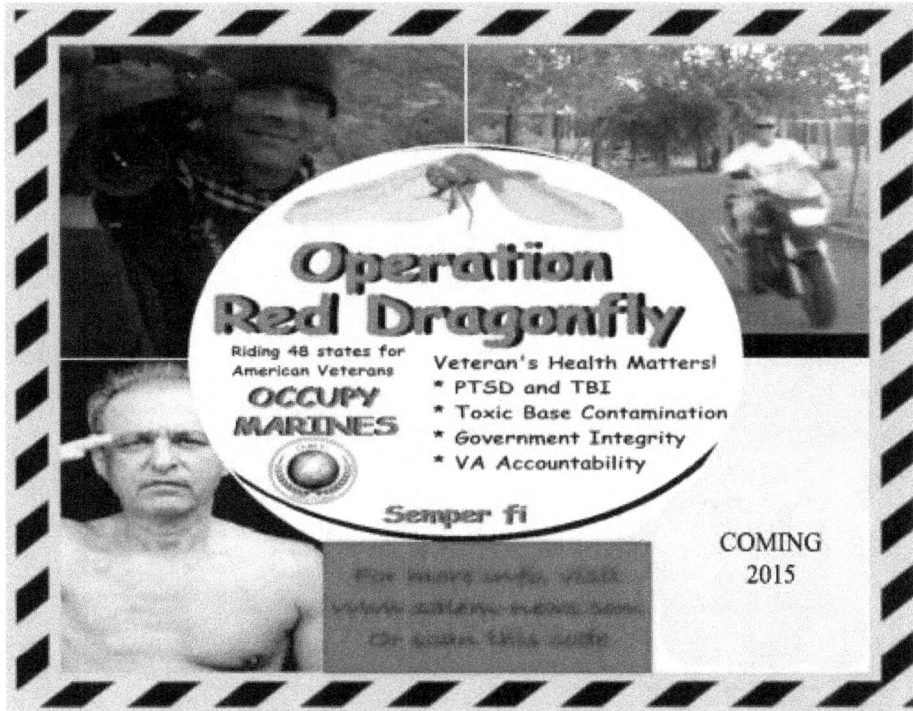

Visit Tim's website at www.globalnewscentre.com

In April 2014 Robert O'Dowd and Tim published a book called Betrayal.

BETRAYAL is the tragic story of toxic chemical exposure of Marines at Marine Corps Air Station El Toro and Marine Corps Base Camp Lejeune, the transport of cocaine into the US on CIA proprietary aircraft at El Toro in a convert operation to support an undeclared war in Nicaragua, the murders those who were a threat to blow the whistle on the illegal narcotrafficking and the blotched government cover-up.

None of the veterans that served aboard these two bases were notified of their exposure to deadly contaminants when it was discovered resulting in both bases earning EPA Superfund status. Many have died without 'connecting the dots' between their killing diseases and military service. The trichloroethylene (TCE) plume at El Toro spreads miles off the former base into Orange County. TCE (a carcinogen) was used at El Toro for decades and contaminated the soil, groundwater and aquifer, cutting a path right through the base wells. The Marine Corps denied ownership of the TCE plume for sixteen years until a lawsuit forced them to accept responsibility.

The documentation of the contaminated base wells at Camp Lejeune and persistence by Marine veterans and their dependents and several Congressmen resulted in the passage of the Janey Ensminger Act in August 2012, covering the cost of medical care by the VA for a number of medical conditions. But, Marines veterans still have to fight for VA disability compensation benefits; most of the claims are denied by the VA and many die before their appeals can be heard; dependent toxic tort claims gather dust in the Navy's Judge Advocate General's office files with no interest in processing them.

The murder (officially a suicide) of Marine Colonel James E. Sabow and other Marines are tied to the use of El Toro's assets to ferry weapons and supplies to the Contra rebel faction in Nicaragua and cocaine into the U.S. to fund an undeclared war in Nicaragua. Relieved from his position pending an investigation of personal misuse of government aircraft, Colonel Sabow demanded a court martial to clear his name of false charges. Until the day before his murder, he had no idea that civilian aircraft used in an NSC covert operation were involved in narcotrafficking. Colonel Sabow had a reputation as a straight arrow Marine and was threat to blow the whistle on those involved in narcotrafficking. The circumstances surrounding his death and the forensic evidence from the crime scene support murder by a government assassination team, crime scene tampering and government cover-up at the highest levels, including a 'doctored autopsy photograph' submitted to a federal district court and in a Defense Department report to Congress to support suicide.

There's no statute of limitations on murder and a formal inquest and reversal of the manner of death to homicide is a threat to the 'shadow government' and powerful individuals who operate outside the rule of law. The Marine Corps has long been the country's premier fighting force. Marines have a long history of service to the country and loyalty to each other. They can be your best friend or your worst enemy. Marines who served honorably and met violent deaths because they knew too much deserved better treatment from a government intent on burying its misdeeds.

BETRAYAL

TOXIC EXPOSURE OF U.S. MARINES, MURDER AND GOVERNMENT COVER-UP

**ROBERT O'DOWD
TIM KING**

Representative Lynn Morris

I was pleased to get this letter from Missouri State Representative Lynn Morris after our 2013 Operation Red Dragonfly. It made me feel special.

Lynn A. Morris
State Representative
District 140

DISTRICT ADDRESS
4101 N Hwy NN
Ozark, MO 65721
417-581-4335

CAPITOL OFFICE
State Capitol
201 West Capitol Avenue
Jefferson City, MO 65101-6806
Tele: (573) 751-2565

E-Mail: lynn.morris@house.mo.go

**MISSOURI HOUSE OF
REPRESENTATIVES**

September 26, 2013

Sheree Evans
1504 W Daniels
Ozark, MO 65721-8851

Sheree,

After reading the CCH article, I want to commend you for your tenaciousness in fulfilling your promise to Tommy through Operation Red Dragonfly.

I am an advocate for our veterans and am spearheading an event in honor of our Viet Nam veterans that will be held in Washington, DC on Memorial Day in 2014.

Your willingness to help give hope to widows throughout the country is deeply impressive and you have my utmost respect. If there is anything I can do to assist Operation Red Dragonfly, please do not hesitate to call me.

Sincerely,

Lynn Morris
State Representative
District 140

COMMITTEES

Appropriations – Health, Mental Health, and Social Services
Economic Development
Health Care Policy
Local Government
Interim Committee on Medicaid Transformation

The Order of the Silver Rose

Due to unforeseeable circumstances The Order of the Silver Rose is temporarily not in working status. The National Director, Gary Chenett, plans to start services again soon.

Below are some correspondence from Gary and the Silver Rose poem.

Subj: RE: AGENT ORANGE
Date: 6/21/2004 5:34:12 PM Central Daylight Time
From: fuzzyfrog
To: EvaSher6
Sent from the Internet (Details)

Sheree;
   You stay on it, You will win,
  I must say I admire your tenacity. You are certainly not a quitter, if we can help let us know.
  When you finally get your settlement, Email me and let's talk about you being possibly a Director for the Silver Rose..
   Keep in touch and let me know how it's going
  Gary

Sheree Evans

From: "fuzzyfrog" <fuzzyfrog
To: <-Vinson
Sent: Wednesday, June 19, 2013 7:21 AM
Subject: Welcome Home from a good friend of Sheree Evans

Hi Jim;
  I am Gary Chenett, a Nam Vet 1967/68 who served with the Big Red One 1st/4th Calvary as a gunner on a APC.
   I am also the National Director of the Order of The Silver Rose.
   We are a group comprised of hundreds of thousands people who are either Veterans who served In Country as you & I did or they are the families of Veterans who have been sickened or killed by the 69 Agent Orange related Dioxins the VA recognizes as caused by the over 22 and 1/2 Million gallons on Agent Orange that was sprayed on us In Country.

Sadly out of the 3.2 Million or more of us that served currently the VA can only find just over 900,000 of us alive. We are dying far to fast and have been for far to long. We are here to go to war against the injustices we have received from the VA and the Government due to AO cancers and sicknesses

During the time that I have been the Director of The Order of The Silver Rose (over 20 years now) we have awarded over 6,000 gratis Silver Rose Medals and awards.
  Sheree has a medal for her husband who died as the result of Agent Orange.

You have a great friend in her.
  I call her Killer Sheree because she was so tenacious in the fight to bring Honors and Recognition to AO Victims.
  It took Tiger over 8 years of fighting the VA to finally receive her Widows Pension (called DIC) for the compensation she was due after her husband gave his life for our Country .
  He died for our Freedoms.

I like you am a AO Victim, Sheree has told me how sick you are and we are willing to try and help you if possible at no charge.
  I have suffered from four AO cancers since 1986. In addition I have had lung cancer twice, (I am trying to recover from my last lung cancer I fought in 2010)
  I have also had Prostate Cancer and Brain Cancer somehow or for some reason God has left me here through these cancers and other combat wounds to continue this fight.

I don't know if we can help you but want you to know that we have people with allot of talent who work with us to try and help Veterans who are having difficulties receiving their compensation.

  I am not a Service Officer but know many good ones if the one you are currently working with is not helping you we would be happy to try.
  Unfortunately we have many slackers working as Service Officers, in fact I went through 7 Service Officers over a 8 year period before I received my first 100% rating. I am now rated at 350% and going for more.

  We never charge for our help and I of course cannot promise I can help you but I will promise you that if you need help you will receive 110% of our efforts to help you.

Feel free to call or email me any time. Always leave a message if you miss me and you will hear back from me within 24 hours.
  If you do not have unlimited calling let me know , then you can send me your phone number and a good time to reach you. We will need about a hour to talk so that I can gather information on your current illness.

I am looking forward to hearing from you.
  I have a Dr's appointment at noon today and then should be home almost always after that.
  God Bless
  Gary Chenett

Sisters of Mercy

Ever after Chapter: Nam Vets with Glio.

I am dedicating the next chapters to all the widows, their stories of our first contacts, and the love of their lives dying from Glio, from Nam. Also the Vietnam Vets who are alive today, having Glio, and making it one day at a time! I want to bring awareness out to the open that our Vietnam Veterans are dealing with aftermath of exposure to Agent Orange, and the Glio, brain cancer so many are suffering with.

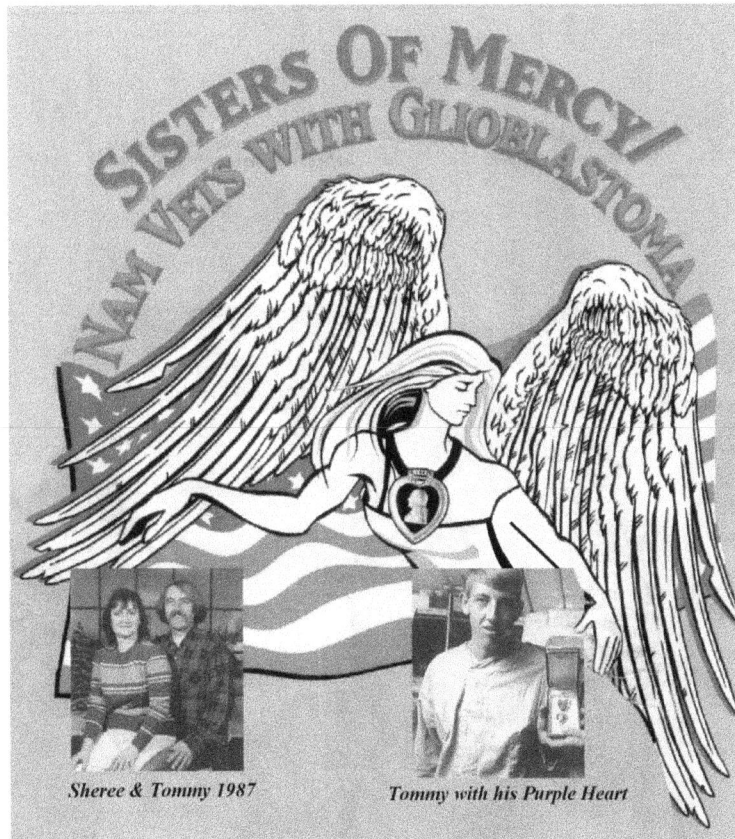

Sheree & Tommy 1987

Tommy with his Purple Heart

The following documents belong to Stewart Hallman's. They show where he won his glio case for disability. I am in hopes this might help others win their case as well.

Stewart Hallman

June 9, 2014

Attention Judge Kerri Millikan,

We are providing additional information for your determination of William S. Hallman's appeal # 319/220A, ~~████████████~~

Specifically, you had directed us to provide you an addendum to the letter from his neuro-oncologist to support her opinion of the relationship of his glioblastoma multiforme (GBM) tumor and the spraying of Agent Orange in Vietnam. This is included in this mailing.

Also included is the summation of the Citation Nr: 1201988 with very important references that are supportive of Agent Orange as a causative carcinogen.

I will summarize the points I feel are supportive of a connection between Agent Orange and the GBM tumor that Mr. Hallman has been diagnosed with:

1. Mr. Hallman is presumed by the VA to have been exposed to Agent Orange during his service time in Viet Nam (May 1969- April 1970) and the massive spraying done in the war. Military records support his time there. Also see Exhibit 1 in his folder – chart of herbicide spray missions and his particular stations in the Delta of Vietnam also support this.

2. Dioxin is a known carcinogen and may be a causative carcinogen at any anatomical site. *(Pursuant to Section 3 of the Agent Orange Act of 1991, Public Law No. ... state,* dioxin is a known carcinogen and may be a causative carcinogen at any anatomical site. ... known carcinogenic *effects of* dioxin *(Agent Orange) at* any anatomical site.*)* Therefore it should not be ruled out that brain cancers are not caused by Agent Orange.

3. The development of Mr. Hallman's GBM tumor cannot be disassociated from his exposure to Agent Orange (refer to point #4)

4. August 2007 opinion of VA's Chief Public Health and Environmental Hazards Officer did not specifically rule out the possibility that the Veteran's glioblastoma was due to Agent Orange exposure or dissociate it from his Agent Orange exposure. (Citation Nr: 1201988 - attached)

5. Also of note: there is no family history of cancers or brain cancers in Mr. Hallman's family on his mother or father's side of the family. Heart and stroke problems are key but there is no cancer.

Thank you for your time and attention to this important matter.

Sincerely,

Janice Hallman on behalf of William Stewart Hallman

I.   MR. HALLMAN WAS EXPOSED TO AO IN HIS ACTIVE SERVICE

        EXHIBIT 1   MAP OF AERIAL HERBICIDE SPRAY MISSIONS

        SERVED 11 MONTHS (MAY 1969 TO APRIL 1970)

                CAN THO – 10 MOS.
                BAC LIEU
                RAC GIA
                CHI LANG

II.   MR. HALLMAN WAS DIAGNOSED WITH GBM

        EXHIBIT 2: LETTER FR. K. B. PETERS, MD, PHD – JULY 24, 2013

        DR. PETERS AVAILABLE BY PHONE AT THIS TIME ~~919-084-01~~

III.   MR. HALLMAN FILED A CLAIM FOR ENTITLEMENT TO SERVICE
       CONNECTION FOR GBM

IV.   MR. HALLMAN'S CLAIM WAS DENIED AND HE TIMELY APPEALED

V.   GBM CANNOT BE DISASSOCIATED FROM MR. HALLMAN'S
       EXPOSURE TO AO

        CASE CITATION NR.: 1201988; DOCKET NO. 08-31-874   *Exhibit 3*

                FINDINGS OF FACT NO. 7: GBM CANNOT BE DISASSOCIATED
                FROM AO EXPOSURE

        EXHIBIT 2:

                EXPOSURE TO AO SIGNIFICANT FACTOR IN CAUSING,
                CONTRIBUTING TO OR AGGRAVATING MR. HALLMAN'S
                BRAIN TUMOR

                IT IS AS LEAST AS LIKELY AS NOT THAT REPEATED HIGH
                LEVEL EXPOSURE TO AO MAY HAVE CAUSED OR
                CONTRIBUTED TO MR. HALLMAN'S BRAIN TUMOR

VI.   MR. HALLMAN SUFFERED PSYCH, PHYSICAL & FINANCIAL LOSS

        EXHIBIT 3: NEUROPSYCH EVAL. BRAIN TUMOR CTR – 12/21/12

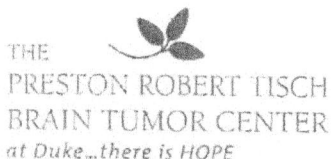

THE
PRESTON ROBERT TISCH
BRAIN TUMOR CENTER
at Duke...there is HOPE

July 24, 2013

Re: William S. Hallman
DOB: 9/26/45

To whom it may concern:

This letter is written on behalf of Mr. Hallman, a current patient of The Preston Robert Tisch Brain Tumor Center at Duke, who filed a claim with the Department of Veteran's Affairs. Mr. Hallman was diagnosed with a left temporal glioblastoma multiforme malignant brain tumor (WHO Grade IV) in April, 2009.

Mr. Hallman has filed a claim with the Department of Veteran's Affairs, stating his brain tumor may have resulted from exposure to Agent Orange during his military service in Vietnam. As a board certified Neuro-Oncologist and brain cancer researcher, it is my opinion that exposure to Agent Orange in Vietnam was a significant factor in causing, contributing to, or aggravating brain tumors in Vietnam veterans.

It is at least as likely as not that repeated high-level exposure to such materials may have caused, contributed to or aggravated brain tumors in patients who are Vietnam Veterans. Please take this information into consideration when reviewing Mr. Hallman's claim. Given that he suffers from a terminal illness, we request that his claim be expedited.

If you have any questions, please feel free to contact our office at ███████████.

Sincerely,

Katherine B. Peters, MD, PhD
Assistant Professor of Medicine
Division of Neurology

KBP/cr

Addendum dated June 5, 2014: As you can see from my above original letter, it is possible that Agent Orange is linked to cancers, such as brain tumors. Given Mr. Hallman's specific exposure to Agent Orange, the duration from exposure to tumor diagnosis, and his very rare diagnosis of glioblastoma multiforme, I believe that it is reasonable to conclude that in the specific case of Mr. Hallman, glioblastoma multiforme and Agent Orange are linked. Currently I am a board certified Neurologist by the ABPN and Neuro-Oncologist by UCNS. I also function as the Program Director of the Neuro-Oncology Fellowship Program. My important component of my research includes evaluations of long-term survivors of primary glioblastoma multiforme and their outcomes. This is relevant to Mr. Hallman's particular case.

Sincerely,

Katherine B. Peters, MD, PhD
Assistant Professor of Neurology

THE PRESTON ROBERT TISCH BRAIN TUMOR CENTER AT DUKE · DUKE UNIVERSITY MEDICAL CENTER
DUMC 3624 · Durham, North Carolina 27710 · tel (919) 684-5301 · fax (919) 684-6674 · www.cancer.duke.edu/btc

80

Appeals for the Federal Circuit (Federal Circuit) has held that the Veterans Dioxin and Radiation Exposure Compensation Standards Act, Pub. L. No. 98- 542, § 5, 98 Stat. 2725, 2727-29 (1984) does not preclude a veteran from establishing service connection with proof of actual direct causation. See Combee v. Brown, 34 F.3d 1039 (Fed. Cir. 1994). In determining whether service connection is warranted for a disability, VA is responsible for determining whether the evidence supports the claim or is in relative equipoise, with the veteran prevailing in either event, or whether a preponderance of the evidence is against the claim, in which case the claim is denied. Gilbert v. Derwinski, 1 Vet. App. 49 (1990); 38 U.S.C.A. § 5107(b) (West 2002); 38 C.F.R. § 3.102 (2011). In this case, the appellant contends that the Veteran's death from glioblastoma multiforme was due to his in-service Agent Orange exposure. Private treatment records show that the Veteran was diagnosed with, and treated for glioblastoma multiforme between 2006 and 2008. His March 2008 death certificate indicates that the cause of his death was congestive heart failure (from which he suffered for hours), due to or as a consequence of vascular overload (from which he had suffered for weeks), and that the underlying cause was glioblastoma multiforme (from which he had suffered more than one year). In order for a veteran to establish service connection on a presumptive basis for a disability that results from exposure to (herbicides) Agent Orange while serving in Vietnam, the disability must be one that is statutorily listed as a presumptive condition. In this case, it is not disputed that the Veteran served in Vietnam during the Vietnam Era. As such, he is presumed to have been exposed to Agent Orange. However, the Board notes that the disabilities that have been positively associated with Agent Orange do not include brain tumors, to include glioblastoma multiforme. See 38 C.F.R. §§ 3.307, 3.309 (2011). Therefore, entitlement to service connection of a presumptive basis is not warranted. However, even if the presumptive service connection statutory provisions are not applicable the appellant may still establish service connection for the veteran's cause of death by competent and probative evidence showing that such disease is somehow related to service (including to Agent Orange exposure therein). See Combee v. Brown. With respect to the etiology of the Veteran's brain tumor, the appellant submitted medical literature and internet articles pertaining to exposure to dioxins (including Agent Orange) and the development of cancer (including brain cancer). The appellant also submitted Board decisions that granted service connection for the cause of the Veteran's death from brain tumors based on exposure to Agent Orange. The appellant also submitted favorable opinions regarding the etiology of the Veteran's glioblastoma multiforme. In this regard, a letter dated on June 20, 2006, shows that Dr. R. D., one of the Veteran's treating oncologists, opined: It is at least as likely as not, that his exposure to Agent Orange and other chemicals while on active duty in Vietnam and Laos are the cause of his multifocal glioblastoma. This opinion is based on the lack of family history in this patient, the lack of any significant other history of cancer, the fact that [the Veteran] was the only member of his family to have served in Vietnam and was exposed to Agent Orange, as well as the other herbicides and pesticides during his service from July 1970 to July 1971. This service is documented on DD from 214. As the enclosed references state, dioxin is a known carcinogen and may be a causative carcinogen at any anatomical site. References are attached. Additionally, in a letter dated on September 19, 2006, Dr. M. E. R., the Veteran's neurologist, stated: I first met [the Veteran] when he presented with seizures on February 3, 2006. The [Veteran] has been under my care as his neurologist since his diagnosis. It is impossible to identify with certainty the cause of [the Veteran's] brain tumors. He has a negative family history of brain tumors specifically, and for cancer of any type. However, he served in Vietnam from July1970 to July 1971, significant exposure to high concentrations of Agent Orange. It is as likely as not that these tumors developed as a result of his exposure to herbicides while on active duty in Vietnam. His military record (DD 214) documents his military service in Vietnam. Research (enclosed) supports the known carcinogenic effects of dioxin (Agent Orange) at any anatomical site. Finally, in a letter dated on October 2, 2006, Dr. W. H. K., one of the Veteran's treating oncologists, noted that the Veteran had been referred to him from a neurosurgeon after he was diagnosed with glioblastoma multiforme of the brain, he had undergone a surgical resection, and under his direction, he was receiving radiation and chemotherapy treatment. Dr. K. opined: It is impossible to identify with certainty the cause of [the Veteran's] brain tumor. He has a negative family history of brain tumor specifically, and for cancer of any type. However, he served in Vietnam from July 1970 to July 1971, and my understanding is that he had significant exposure to high-concentrations of Agent Orange. It is as likely as not that this tumor developed as a result of his exposure to herbicides while on active duty in Vietnam. His military record (DD214) documents his military service in Vietnam. Research supports the known carcinogenic effects of dioxin (Agent Orange) at any anatomical site. Also of record is an August 20, 2007 Memorandum in which VA's Chief Public Health and Environmental Hazards Officer, in response to an undated memorandum from the Director of Compensation and Pension Service, provided an opinion regarding the etiology of the Veteran's glioblastoma multiforme due to exposure to herbicides. According to L. R. D.: The recently-released Institute of Medicine (IOM), National Academy of Sciences (NAS), report on herbicides used in Vietnam, Veterans and Agent Orange, Update 2006 (available on line at www.nas.edu) concluded that there was inadequate or insufficient evidence to determine whether an association exists between exposure to herbicides and cancers of brain and nervous system (IOM report, prepublication copy, page 10). This assessment was based on information obtained from extensive review of the scientific and medical literature. The VA by law and precedent gives a lot of weight to the IOM findings on health effects from exposure to herbicides used in Vietnam. Therefore, at this time, in our opinion it is possible that the Veteran's glioblastoma multiforme was due to exposure to herbicides used in Vietnam but we cannot state that it is likely or as likely as not that the disease resulted from such exposure. Further, in an August 28, 2007 Advisory opinion, the Director of Compensation and Pension Service, based on the August 20, 2007 opinion provided by the Under Secretary for Health, and review of the evidence in its entirety found that "there is no reasonable possibility that the Veteran's glioblastoma multiforme was the result of his exposure to herbicides in Vietnam." In weighing the evidence of record, the Board finds that the three favorable opinions with respect to etiology of the Veteran's brain cancer to be highly probative and will be given much evidentiary weight because they were provided by his treating oncologists and neurologists, who were familiar with his medical history and who also provided well-supported rationales for their stated conclusions. Further, the Board observes that in his August 2007 opinion, VA's Chief Public Health and Environmental Hazards Officer for did not specifically rule out the possibility that the Veteran's glioblastoma was due to Agent Orange exposure or dissociate

it from his Agent Orange exposure. Rather, he opined that it was
"possible" that the Veteran's brain tumor resulted from Agent Orange
exposure but could not state "that it is likely or as likely as not."
Therefore, the Board finds that the evidence is in equiopoise as to the
etiological relationship between the Veteran's fatal gliosbastoma
multiforme and his Agent Orange exposure in Vietnam. Accordingly,
resolving all reasonable doubt in the appellant's favor, the Board
concludes that service connection for the cause of the Veteran's death
is warranted. 2. Accrued Benefits Although a veteran's claims
terminate with his death, certain survivors of a deceased veteran are
eligible to receive payments from VA of accrued benefits based upon the
deceased veteran's statutory entitlement to such benefits. Accrued
benefits are defined as periodic monetary benefits payable under laws
administered by VA to which an individual was entitled at death under
existing ratings or decisions, or those based on evidence in the file
at date of death. 38 U.S.C.A. § 5121 (West 2002); see Landicho v.
Brown, 7 Vet. App. 42, 47 (1994). There are various threshold
requirements that an appellant must meet in order to pursue an accrued
benefits claim. One such requirement is that applications for accrued
benefits must be filed within one year after the date of death. 38
U.S.C.A. § 5121 (c); 38 C.F.R. § 3.1000 (c). A claim for DIC is deemed
to include a claim for accrued benefits. 38 C.F.R. § 3.1000.
Another requirement is that a veteran must have had a claim pending at
the time of his death for such benefits or else be entitled to them
under an existing rating or decision. See Jones v. West, 136 F.3d
1296, 1300 (Fed. Cir. 1998); Zevalkink v. Brown, 102 F.3d 1236, 1241-
1242 (Fed. Cir. 1996) (a consequence of the derivative nature of the
surviving spouse's entitlement to a veteran's accrued benefits claim is
that, without the veteran having a claim pending at the time of death,
the surviving spouse has no claim upon which to derive his or her own
application). The provisions of 38 C.F.R. § 3.1000(d)(5) define a
claim for VA benefits pending on the date of death as a claim "filed"
with VA that had not been finally adjudicated by VA on or before the
date of death. In addition, as noted, accrued benefits may only be
awarded on the basis of the evidence in the file at the Veteran's date
of death. See 38 C.F.R. § 3.1000(a). "Evidence in the file at date
of death" means evidence in VA's possession on or before the date of
the veteran's death, even if such evidence was not physically located
in the VA claims folder on or before the date of death. 38 C.F.R. §
3.1000(d)(4). In this case, the record shows that in March 2006, the
Veteran filed a claim of entitlement to service connection for brain
cancer due to herbicide exposure. Such claim was denied by the RO in a
June 2006 decision. The Veteran submitted a VA Form 9 in October 2007,
thus perfecting an appeal with regard to the matter. The Veteran died
in March 2008. Thus, at the time of the Veteran's death, he had a
pending appeal of entitlement to service connection for glioblastoma
multiforme, to include as due to Agent Orange exposure. A review of
the evidence deemed to be of record at the time of the Veteran's March
2008 death reflects an approximate balance of positive and negative
evidence. In this regard, the Chief Public Health and Environmental
Hazards Officer August 2007 opinion did not specifically rule out the
possibility that the Veteran's glioblastoma multiform was due to Agent
Orange exposure. Further, in 2006, the Veteran's private treating
oncologists and neurologists opined that it was at least as likely as
not that the Veteran's exposure to Agent Orange caused his multifocal
glioblastoma. As previously noted, these opinions are accorded
considerable weight in light of the fact that they were provided by
the Veteran's treating oncologists and neurologists who was familiar

with the Veteran's medical history and provided well-supported
rationales for their stated conclusions.   Therefore, resolving all
reasonable doubt in the appellant's favor, the Board concludes that
service connection for glioblastoma multiform should be granted for
the purpose of payment of accrued benefits.   (CONTINUED ON NEXT
PAGE)   ORDER Entitlement to service connection for the cause of the
Veteran's death is granted.   Entitlement to service connection for
glioblastoma multiforme for accrued benefits is granted.
_____ H. SCHWARTZ Veterans Law
Judge, Board of Veterans' Appeals Department of Veterans Affairs

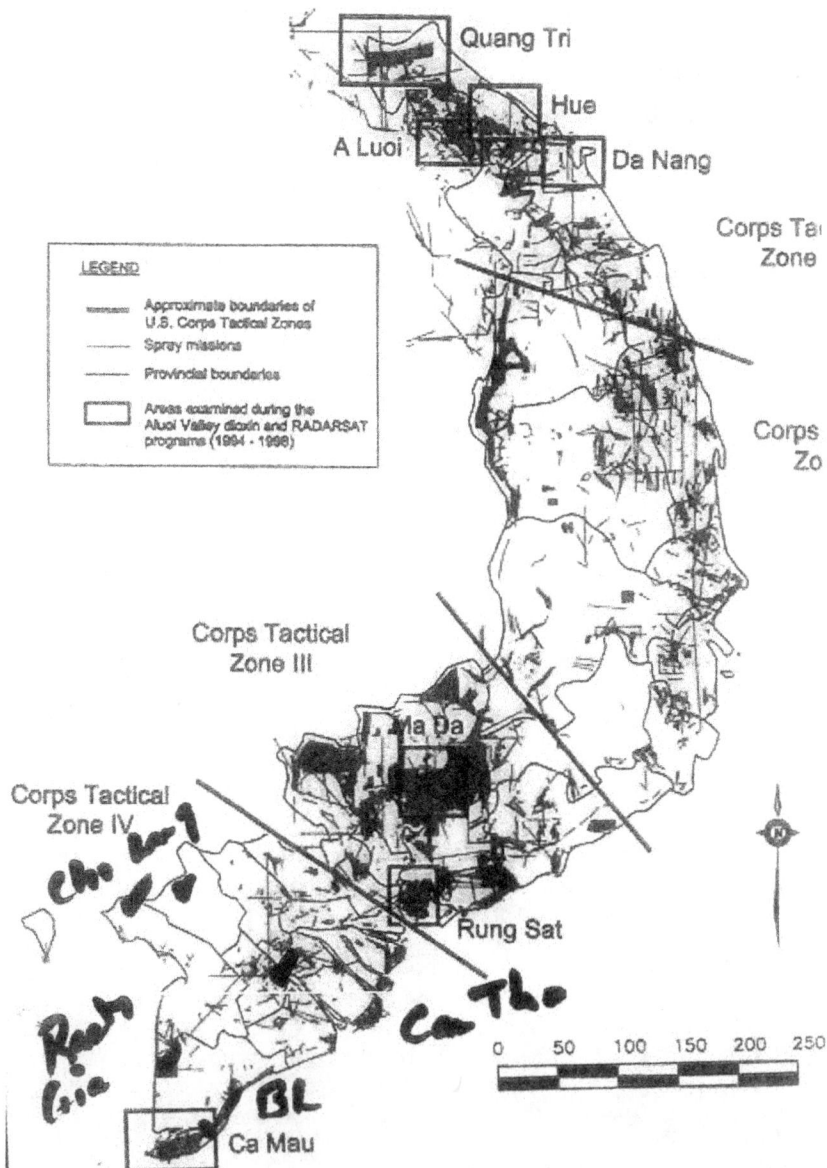

Aerial herbicide spray missions in southern Viet Nam.
(Source: U.S. Dept. of the Army).

This not only affects the war veteran, but his loving supportive wife as well. She deals with so many daily tasks, her family, her children and their needs, while always being there for her husband. She loves her husband and thinks of his comfort, his emotions and much more while she prays for the strength she needs from God and His company of Angels to help her cope with the cards she's been dealt.

Following are the first contacts that I received either via US mail or email and many phone calls. I didn't realize that I had such an impact on winning for Glio, but I proved benefit of doubt can come out on top.

My case opened doors to help these widows with their cases. I really felt for myself, being just a typical middle aged hard working wife, that I had accomplished so much more than I could ever imagine. I didn't finish High School, nor go to College, but I always enjoyed reading the news, and about our military.

I dreamed that one day my ambitions would take flight, I kept the promise I made Tommy. I felt an inner peace when I won, I was proud of myself. I achieved so much and had no idea of the full impact I would have on others. It has made me more involved in what I want to do. One of those accomplishments was to finish writing this book, so I can bring awareness to everyone involved.

Here are these brave, strong women's stories.

Sher Green

Sher was the first widow to contact me after I won my case.

Sher Green

Sheree Evans

From:
To: "Sheree Evans"
Sent: Saturday, August 11, 2012 2:22 AM
Subject: Sher Green

Hi Sheree,

"Good job Sheree, I am with you regarding the Glioblastoma Brain Cancer and I will never give up the fight for all Veterans who have already died from it or will die from it. My husband, Joseph Green died from it on 2/14/12 and I started my battle with the VA. It is all about Justice and I am a fighter, so they have a real battle on their hands because I refuse to give up, I will fight until I win! I would like to thank you for the courage you have portrayed for the last 8 years of your battle with the VA and thank you for your encouragement and help recently. We are so much alike and between the two of us, I am quite sure, we can make a difference in the future for other widowed women who have suffered the loss of their Vietnam Vet husbands! Our own Government did this one too! Trust?? I will fight and I will Win!!!"

Rickey Pramov

Mrs. Evans:

I read an article on the internet about your fight with the Va. and your success in proving it came from Agent Orange. My husband was in Nam in 1964-65 and agent orange, blue, green and white were all stored there and loaded onto the planes. But the Va. will not his recognize cancer. Five years ago he was also diagnosed with walderstrom macroglobulinemia, but they claim it is not serious enough. If you would be so kind to give us any help, we would be ever so grateful.

Thank you,

& God Bless!

Rickey Pramov

Sheree Evans

From:	<rickeyp1
To:	<evasher6
Sent:	Monday, September 03, 2012 5:34 PM
Subject:	Re: agent orange exposure-Glioblastoma

Sheree

First things first I want to thank you for answering my letter. You are the first to do that. I need advice on how to get help from the VA. My husband was diagnosed 6 years ago with **Waldenstrom's macroglobulinemia** and last year with glioblastoma stage IV. He was stationed in Qui Nhon in 1964-65. They stored and transport all the rainbow agents. There was not any plant life around their air strip. We have a letter from his oncologist stating it is possible it is from Nham but the Va claims agent orange does not cause glio. So anything you can tell me or lead in the right direction would be very helpful.

A week ago we found out the cancer is growing again. Last Sept 21 he had surgery then 6 weeks of radiation with daily chemo. Then monthly chemo. We are now facing another surgery on Sept 11 and we are entering a trial. They will remove the tumor, treat it then implant it in his abdomen, 24 hours later they will remove it. They think it will make his body creat antibodies to fight the cancer. Sorry to dump this on you and it has probably stirred up some bad memories. But thanks for listening.

Thank you
Rickey

Johnnie & Pauline Bonham

Johnnie, Pauline & Brian
Minot, North Dakota 1964 – Lived in an 8 x 40 trailer and were so happy.

Johnnie & Pauline 1997

Johnnie - Asheville Airport, NC – September 27th, 1966
Leaving for Nha Trang, Vietnam.

Johnnie 1967 on the runway at Nha Trang, Vietnam Air Station.

January 4, 2013

Johnnie F. Bonham and Pauline Bonham

I met Johnny when he was introduced to me by my best friend. I had gone all through high school with his sister but had never met him. He was home on leave from the Air Force for Christmas for 30 days, in route from Homestead, FL to Minot, North Dakota. I liked him instantly - huge smile, good sense of humor, good looking, good personality and 2 years older than me. We married a year later on January 27, 1962 and returned to Minot, North Dakota.

From there we transferred to Homestead, FL for a year where he received orders for Vietnam. I returned to my hometown for that year with our 4 year old son. Johnny was stationed in Vietnam from Sept. 27, 1966 to Sept. 26, 1967. He was stationed at Nha Trang Air Station where he was an aircraft electrician. He repaired the airplanes, having his hands and face continually down in the electrical wiring on the planes. He told me many times that he was exposed to agent orange. (the VA has acknowledged that he was exposed to agent orange)

In 2005 he began to lose weight rapidly (but no other symptoms that were obvious except memory problems a few months before) and on October 28, he had a near fatal seizure. That is when doctors found the GBM brain tumor, stage 4. He had had it for a number of years. It was inoperable. He went through chemo and radiation and lived 10 months. I took care of him at home. He crossed over to eternal life on August 27, 2006. He was the most patriotic person I have ever met. *And still, saying all this, I cry!*

I did not file a claim until June 2011. We had been married 44+ years and I found it hard to deal with. That is, until I read the report on internet by Sheree Evans and her claim results. I had told my daughter ever since her dad died that I believed it had to have been agent orange. Why? Because he also had all these other things caused by agent orange:

1. Diabetes - on medication starting 1989
2. Anxiety (took Valium)
3. Tingling and numbness in both hands (complained of this often)
4. Hypertension
5. Ringing in the ears
6. Glioblastoma multiforme brain tumor, stage 4 when found

I want what is fair for myself and my family. I am determined to keep "my feet to the fire." It is what Johnny would have wanted.

About myself:

I worked for years as an accounting tech and later as a church secretary. I have had my own class at the detention center (jail) downtown in Asheville, NC for 5 years, every Tuesday teaching 10 inmate ladies. God enables me to do it. To Him be all the glory.

My favorite color is probably red or rose. Hey, I love purple also. I love to do jigsaw puzzles, crosswords, word jumble, scrabble, and sudoku. And I love to read. My birthday is May 16 and my favorite song is Matt Redman's "10,000 Reasons."

I have found that God has become my "husband" and my truest friend. I will always always always miss my Johnny, every day. But God. He gives perfect peace.

Pauline Boxham

a christmas gift

* Johnny:
B-day: 12-24-1937
Date of: 08-27-2006
Death
age in Vietnam: 29
age when he crossed
over: 68

* His mother spelled it
Johnnie on his birth certificate.
Thats how the AF knew him.

Med. 33: 780-785) and others reporting SMR, PMR, SRR values, as well as OR
values, as unity (1.0) for no increased risk or incidence over the
expected, two (2.0) for twice the risk or incidence, etc. In other words,
multiplying the SMR or PMR ratio by 100, etc., is not done. This convention
results in greater consistency between Smr, PMR, and OR values.

Introduction ~ 5
Vietnam veterans, without consideration for that subgroup with the highest
probability of being significantly exposed to Agent Orange, in which less
than a doubling of the background incidence of dioxin-related health
effects was observed, it may be assumed that the actual level of risk
actually was greater than a doubling of the background incidence for that
subgroup of veterans having the highest probability of significant
exposures. This is due to the dilution effect resulting from including
Vietnam veterans in the study population who were not significantly
exposed
along with those who did experience significant exposures. Studies are
presented below that demonstrate that a subgroup of Vietnam veterans
most
likely to have been exposed to Agent Orange (in addition to those who
directly sprayed or handled herbicides) can be identified. The level of
dioxin-related health effects experienced by this subgroup also has been
determined to be much higher than that found in studies examining the
total
group of Vietnam veterans without regard for potential exposure.
5. Studies reported below show that the greatest increased relative risk
of cancers due to dioxin exposure are detected in exposed groups only
twenty (20) years or more after the exposure (latency period). Therefore,
for Vietnam veterans whose exposures occurred after 1964, it would be
premature to draw negative inferences of causation on the basis of the
limited studies of veterans available in 1984, as the courts attempted to
do in the previous Agent Orange litigation. For example, in 1984, a
preliminary Air Force study was used as one basis for concluding there
were
no excess cancer risks among Vietnam veterans. This study evaluated
cancer
risks among pilots who conducted Agent Orange spray missions, where
the
majority conducted spray missions during 1968 and 1969. Since the
preliminary Air Force study only evaluated the health status of these
pilots as of 1982, the approximate latency period from exposure in Vietnam
to 1982 only would have been fourteen to fifteen years, an insufficient
period for cancers to develop. New Air Force studies on the same pilots'
health status as of 1987, however, now show elevated rates of all cancers,
as well as elevated skin cancer rates and other serious health effects,

Doug and Bonnie Walkley

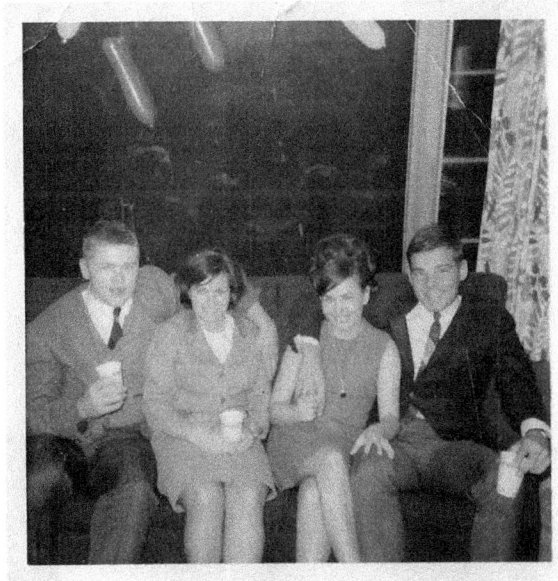

Our engagement picture...we are the couple on the right.

Doug's Army picture.

Our Family

My wonderful husband that our children missed
growing up, and my grandchildren will never know

I met my husband Doug in the summer of 1964. His Father introduced us because his father worked with my Dad and he liked me. Doug asked me out and we spent the entire senior year of high school going steady then to the senior prom. He was my everything!

After high school, Doug, had gone on to college in Michigan. He ended up dropping out and bingo...the draft got him. He went to Vietnam in January 1968. I had gotten pregnant with our first child before he left, so we met in Honolulu on his R & R and got married.

He spent that year in Vietnam in the infantry out in the jungles, fighting for our country. When he returned we spent the remainder of his active duty at Ft. Benning, GA.

Doug was a strong and healthy man. When he was 37 he had a seizure and was diagnosed with Glioblastoma stage 4 brain cancer. It was inoperable. He was given only 3 months to live.

We were such a young couple and it tipped our lives upside down. The only thing I had was a pamphlet stating that Blood type A males with a chemical spray exposure were at high risk for this type of cancer.

Our second child was born (1973) with hyaline membrane disease, she has had multiple problems with bones, eyes, aches and pains, and migraines. I can't help but believe that Agent Orange had something to do with this. There was no history on either side of his family.

I certainly pray that in my lifetime that the truth be told. My children will continue my research.

God Bless,
Bonnie

Rudy and Margie Morris

Rudy's Story

Rudy's Story

Rudy was born in Oakland, CA on Feb. 13, 1952.

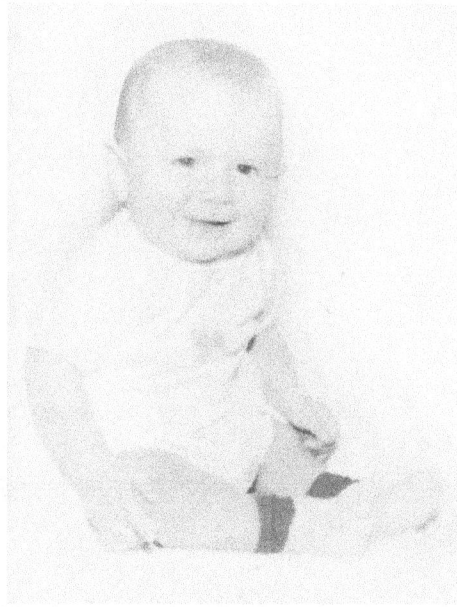

Rudy grew up the middle child of seven. His father was never in the picture. He was murdered when Rudy was 11 years old in a Bar fight that he tried to break up; he was only 38 years old. Rudy's Grandfather died at 47 years old of heart failure. Rudy never met any of his Dad's family, they all lived in Texas.

Rudy risked his life to go back into a burning tank that had been blown up to rescue a fellow soldier, yet the Lt. said he was just doing his duty, so he would not put him in for a Purple Heart.

He talked about all of the spraying that was done over them, at the time I didn't know it was Agent Orange or other Dioxins that may have been sprayed on them. They used to spray their bodies with DDT to keep the mosquitoes from eating them alive. He talked about all of the huge spiders in Nam, he was deathly afraid of spiders.

He injuries in Nam, he was stabbed in the foot with a knife, playing a game. He also got some shrapnel in his stomach, when a tank exploded.

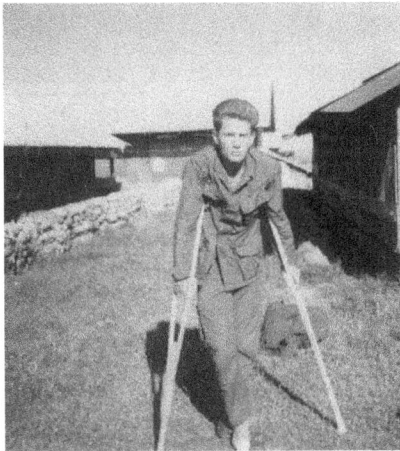

July 1971, he came home from Nam and we were married on July 17, 1971. We were the first in our town to be married in the town's community park, which was right next to the Rail Road Station. We had to time the trains to know when to have our ceremony. Almost our whole town was there for us. Some of Rudy's relatives drove up from Bay Area.

But shortly afterwards, he started thinking he was in Nam again and started guarding our house. Then one day while on one of his walks. One day he called me and told me "Gooks" were everywhere in the bushes and wanted me to bring his gun, that there were enemy everywhere.

Mona, our oldest daughter and I walked down the road to get him and walked him home. This episode was very upsetting. I no longer wanted him walking alone, but he did not want anyone walking with him.

In November 2011, they told us no more treatments and he started Hospice at our house. Marc came home from NJ and helped me care for Rudy, along with what the other son in-laws and our girls could do for him. It was very hard on all of us. So much was left unsaid that still bothers me today.

He lived 4 weeks after Hospice began; he died on Dec. 10, 2011, surrounded by family. All three of the girls, their husbands and all 7 grandkids were with him when he took his last breaths. He hadn't talked to us in days, but I knew he could hear what we were saying to him. I had the radio playing for him all day that day, when the song, "There Will Be a Day" started playing, I knew deep down in my heart that the end was near. Rudy took his last breath when the song ended.

The Hanford Patrol and VFW, Richland, WA did his Memorial service. It was a beautiful Memorial and when they called his number out on the radio from the Patrol car, we all lost it. It would be the last time his number would be called.

Rudy we miss you so much!

Frank and Kathy Josenhans

4-Ever

Our Wedding Day

September 2009

November 2010

Before GBM4

After GBM4

Frank and I met in 1991 and it was a 2nd marriage for us both. It was love at first sight. He was the man I dreamed about when I was a little girl.

We combined our children (step) and made one family unit. We were married for 18 years but together longer.

That nasty cancer was around for a few years before we knew he had one. There were some changes in his personality and we all (family and friends) noticed something was different. Who would have thought it was a brain tumor.

He was a Navy Diver and was aboard many ships around the world.

I have a letter he wrote (he dictated) about his service. He was drafted in 1970.

Kathy

THE DAYTONA BEACH
NEWS-JOURNAL
NEWS-JOURNALONLINE.COM

HOME OF THE WORLD'S MOST FAMOUS BEACH

FRANK E. JOSENHANS III

Obituary

Frank E. Josenhans, III, left us to be a warrior for God on Thursday, January 27, 2011 at the age of 58 after losing his battle with brain cancer. We were blessed and privileged to share the same path he walked in his journey from this earth to everlasting peace. Frank was born at the Southernmost Point in Key West, FL on December 3, 1952. He was the adored husband of Kathy-Lynn Carroll-Josenhans; beloved son of Frank E. and Thelma K. Josenhans; brother to Guy A. Josenhans; loving father to Mary Lynn Lyon, Christina A. Millar and Steven W. Priff, II; loving grandfather to Frank C. Meleca and Jasmine M. Vaglica. He leaves several nieces, nephews and friends he considered family including Eddie, Kurt, Bill and Paul. Frank was a Vietnam Era Navy Diver for six years. He was a Law Enforcement Officer for Daytona Beach Police Department before retiring from the Volusia County Sheriff's office in 2000 as a Deputy Sheriff. Frank was employed by Volusia Motorcycle Training as a Rider Coach before his illness. He had the love of adventure in his heart and lived for the next motorcycle trip. Frank will be remembered for his kind heart, love of life and his awe-inspiring spirit. He will be missed dearly by many. A Life Celebration will be held at 12 Noon, Saturday, February 5, 2011 at the VFW Post 3282, 5810 S. Williamson Blvd., Port Orange. To share a memory with the family, visit www.BaldwinCremation.com. Arrangements entrusted to Baldwin Brothers Cremation Society, New Smyrna Beach.

Guest Book

"Somehow I know your Christmas will be brighter than..."
- *Robert Carroll Jr.*

View   Sign

More Photos

View all 7 photos

Robert & Cynthia Oeleis

Robert passed away February 22, 2013. We were married on June 24, 2000 and I stayed with him to the end. It was rough.

The VA promised him help even a social worker, but they didn't come through.

We sat around the table and cried for two days. We felt the VA basically put a toe tag on him and sent him home to die, so we deiced to fight back.

We got a ramp in three months, and a power chair, because he couldn't walk any more. What's so ironic is they approved *adapting housing* so we got a handicapped bathroom. Then they also approved 2,000,000 but since they knew he was dying they sent a letter saying he was disapproved.

I feel for the men and woman who are serving this country today, and what they have to do just to be heard.

Cindy

Letters from Other Wives and Widows

Denise Layer

1-14-13

Dear Mrs Evans,

I recently read the article "VA Links Brain Cancer to Agent Orange Exposure in recent court decision" (Feb. 17, 2011, KV3 News).

My story is remarkably similar to your own. My husband, Dennis, a Vietnam veteran, was diagnosed with a glioblastoma in Feb of 1996 and died a horrible death in July of the same year.

As he fought his disease, he also tried relentlessly to begin processing his claim to the V.A., that his condition was caused by exposure and consumption of Agent Orange... in the air he breathe, the water he drank, and the jungles he traveled. This was his firm belief!

During his last days, he made me promise to continue the fight. After years of hoplessness & denials of my appeals, your story has given me renewed passion

(2)

to my beloved husband, Dennis.
I've raised my children
virtually alone... never remarried.
Since their coming of age, I
have lost my social security benefits.
After being out of the work force
for so long, I have been unable to
find a job to make ends meet. Can
you PLEASE help me?
    I can be reached at:

Thanking you in advance,
            Denise Fayer

Diane Swisher

Hi Sheree!

Thanks again for all the information. I am so confused on what to do. My VA rep is telling me to go straight to an attorney. She has recommended one and I am going to talk to her. It is hard to know what to do. It has helped to hear your story.

I am from Archbold Ohio. It is a small town about 40 miles west of Toledo. My husband was in Viet Nam in 1969-1970. He says he remembers the planes going over and being sprayed with Agent Orange at least twice. He had his first symptom on June 26th last year. He was in the hospital for a week while they ran tests. They found something on his brain did a biopsy and found the cancer. It seems like a whirlwind after that. We went to Cleveland Clinic twice for 2nd opinions on his treatments. He did all his treatments in Toledo. He did the 7 weeks of daily radiation and was taking Temodar for the chemo. He didn't react well to that so went on Avastin treatments. He had a seizure in January which really knocked him down. He was unconscious for about 4 days. He ended up in the nursing home for 3 weeks to get his mobility and strength back. He kept fighting though and made it home. He kept getting weaker and more confused. The first part of May he had a doctor appointment and decided it was time to stop treatments. The doctor agreed and the next day Hospice came in. He was around for 3 more weeks. He died almost 11 months from the day of his first symptom.

Bill was a very smart man. Several months before he was diagnosed he was reading about Agent Orange and all the effects that it had on the veterans. He told me about it. It was almost like he knew something was coming. He also told me there were not very many Viet Nam vets left.

When I read the stories on Facebook they are almost identical to Bill's. It just doesn't make any sense that the VA does not recognize this.

I hope you are doing well. I am sure you miss your husband very much every day. He sounds like a very good and loving man.

Take care
Diane

Jackie Freeman

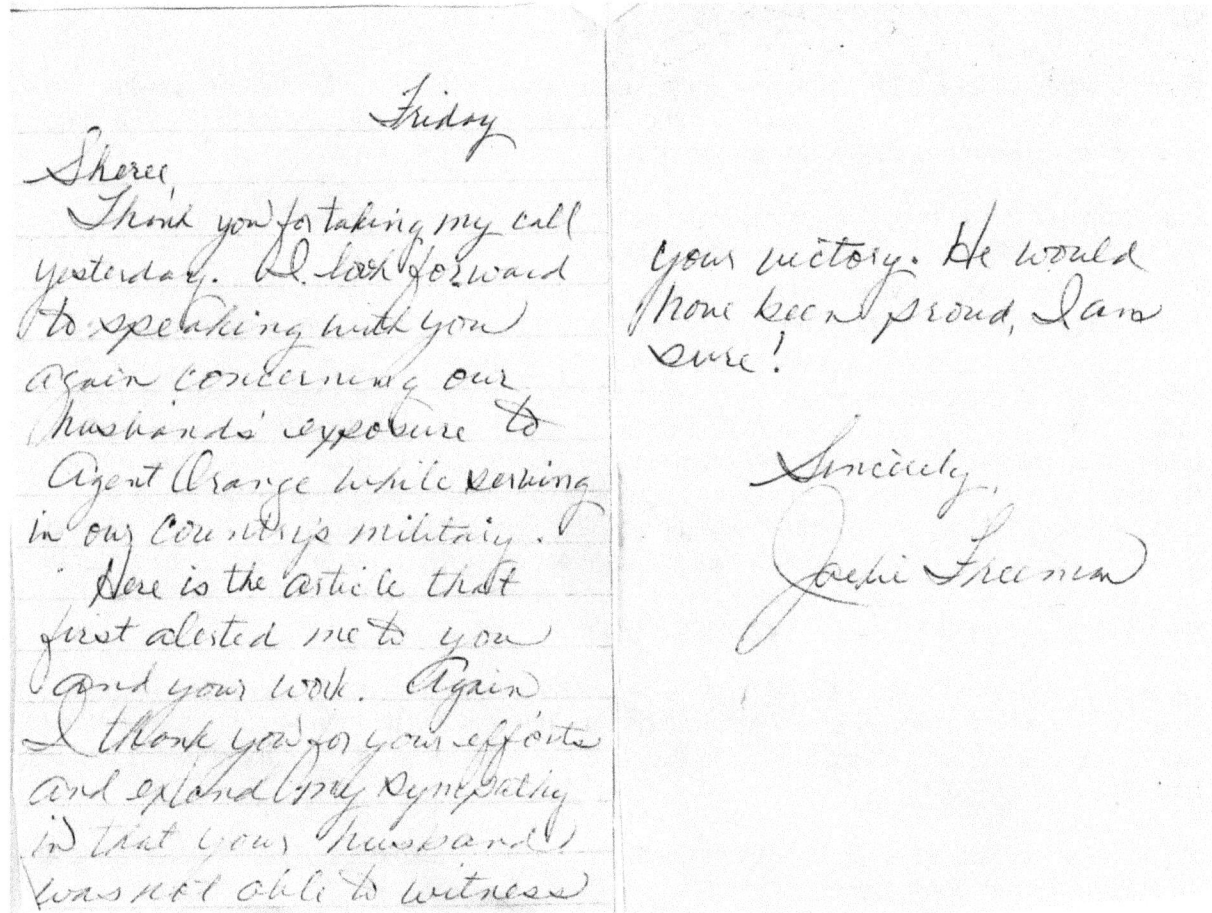

Friday

Sheree,

Thank you for taking my call yesterday. I look forward to speaking with you again concerning our husbands' exposure to Agent Orange while serving in our country's military.

Here is the article that first alerted me to you and your work. Again I thank you for your efforts and extend my sympathy in that your husband was not able to witness your victory. He would have been proud, I am sure!

Sincerely,

Jackie Freeman

Below is an article Jackie sent to me that was written about my case.

Thank you, Jackie.

The Award Winning
UAW LOCAL 600 FACTS

UAW Local 600

"A history to be proud of, a tradition to carry on." — Bernie Ricke

POSTMASTER
Send only mailing label of undeliverable copies with Form 3579 attached to Local 600, UAW, 10550 Dix Avenue, Dearborn, Michigan 48120.

MAY – JUNE 2011

VOL. 73 – NO. 3

Bill Bisbing, Chairman

VA LINKS BRAIN CANCER TO AGENT ORANGE EXPOSURE

It is notoriously difficult for veterans to get their disabilities connected to their military service-even when the connection is apparent. In this unique case, the Department of Veterans Affairs was made to concede a very important connection and gave justice to a struggling widow.

Mrs. Sheree Evans is the surviving spouse of Vietnam Veteran, Edward T. Evans, who passed away from Glioblastoma Multiforme (GM), or more commonly known as brain cancer, in March of 2003. Since this time, Sheree has fought for widow's benefits from the Department of Veterans Affairs (VA) for her husband's cause of death as a result of Agent Orange exposure (Board of Veterans' Appeals, Docket No.05-00 201/U.S. Court of Appeals for Veterans Claims, Vet. App. No. 06-2190). While Mr. Evans was presumed to have been exposed to Agent Orange during his service in the Vietnam War, one of the most challenging obstacles for Sheree was showing that his exposure to Agent Orange caused the development of brain cancer. VA had consistently maintained that brain cancer is not on their list of Agent Orange-related disabilities, and, as a result, that there is no medical link for the development of this specific cancer to Agent Orange Exposure.

Sheree's long struggle against VA took her to the board of Veterans' Appeals, the highest level of the Veterans Administration's appeal process. Once she had been denied there, Sheree appealed her case to the Court of Appeals for Veterans Claims. There she was successful in getting the final decision by VA vacated because VA had used an independent medical opinion as evidence. The VA then ordered another medical opinion which determined that there was no research into the relationship between GM and Agent Orange. Sheree countered with a medical assessment which argued that there was an abundance of research into the relationship between GM and Agent Orange. The Board of Veterans' Appeals then decided that the evidence in favor and against were in equal weight and applied the benefit of the doubt rule and on January 26th, 2011 granted Sheree's claim.

According to Court documents, Sheree had fought for service connection for the cause of her husband's death for almost eight years, based on a promise that she made to him before his death. Sheree plans to write a book in honor of Edward that commemorates his life, his struggle with Post Traumatic Stress Disorder as a result of his combat experience in Vietnam. GM is a highly aggressive form of brain cancer which, when left untreated, usually results in death in less than three months. GM has been widely researched and recent studies indicate that there is an increasing prevalence of brain cancers as a result of exposure to toxins (IOM, 2008). Studies of the dioxin TCDD, the main dioxin in Agent Orange, in laboratory animals have

Jackie Ludwig

Sent: Thursday, January 03, 2013 1:56 PM
Subject: GBM 4

Sheree - we have just discovered your website, story, Facebook and email. My husband was diagnosed August 5th, brain surgery in Tampa August 6th, and a second brain surgery August 29th at Duke University. We are on the second part of a clinical trial and have just now been able to take a breathe and start to look into all of this. One of our long time Army friends advised going to the VA clinic..we have our first appointment on January 16th and starting to get information together for them.

Do you have any suggestions, comments, directives – anything that might help us when we talk to them. We just had an infusion today and our oncologist has only seen 2 or 3 cases over the last years and was not interested in helping us with a letter. Do you of any place we can get documentation of AO, and if there is a doctor who would give us a letter that states..."as likely as not related to Agent Orange.." the wonderful VA counselor I met with initially advised that the letter must have this statement with the notations. We will continue to try to get our primary care physician, and our doctor at Duke University to help with this letter.

Thanks for you time and hope to hear from you...

Jackie Ludwig

p.s. I did send an email to rgmorris @ clearwire.net – asking for information....are you familiar with this person?
Best regards,

Wilma Cox

DEAR MRS. EVANS,   05/28/2012

    MY NAME IS WILMA McCAIN.
I LIVE IN ST. LOUIS, MO. I SAW ON LINE
THAT YOU WON YOUR CASE AGAINST THE VA.
I HAVE BEEN TRYING TO DO THE SAME THING
SINCE 1992 WHEN MY 42 YEAR OLD
VIETNAM VETERAN DIED FROM GLIOBLASTOMA
MULTIFORME, IT IS ON HIS DEATH
CERTIFICATE. I HAVE 2 CHILDREN WHO
AT THE TIME WERE 13, AND 9. I PUT IN A
CLAIM RIGHT AFTER HIS DEATH. I DO
HAVE AN ATTORNEY, BUT SO FAR HE
HAS DONE NOTHING, EXCEPT GET ME A
HEARING, AND TRY TO SHOW THAT THE
SEIZURE DISORDER WAS CAUSED FROM
PTSD.

109

-2.

THAT WAS NOV 17TH 2011.
HAUN'T HEARD ANYTHING SINCE THEN.
NOW THAT YOU WON THIS, MAYBE I HAVE A
CHANGE. I NEVER RECEIVED ANYTHING
AFTER HE DIED, BECAUSE THEY DID NOT
PUT HIM ON TOTAL DISABILITY UNTIL 4
YEARS BEFORE HE DIED. EVEN THOUGH

12 YEARS BEFORE THAT. HE COULDN'T WORK
     IF YOU COULD HELP ME WITH INFORMA-
TION, I WOULD REALLY APPRECIATE IT.
I'M SO HAPPY FOR YOU

                              SINCERLY
                              Wilma McCain

Jim Vinson

Good Morning Sheree,

I obtained your email address on the Forum from David Barker.

First, my condolences on the loss of your husband, Ed
Second, congratulations on your victory against the VA on appeal.

I am a Vietnam veteran who was diagnosed with GM in August 2011. I have put a claim into the VA but was denied, I have sent in my Notice of Disagreement and I⊐$B!G⊐(Bm waiting for their response.

I will probably have the same issues you had during your battles with the VA, the first issue will be to show a link that Agent Orange
caused the development of brain cancer. Can you provide me with a list of the other issues that I will face? Can you also assist me with the counter points to their list of issues?

Any help would be greatly appreciated. Thank you.

Sincerely

Jim

* * *

Sent: Tuesday, July 09, 2013 5:24 AM
Subject: RE: Hello-GM Information
Thanks for your concern and prayers I still owe you a story

Im working with Gary on my claim The 4th was good my son is a lt. In the local volunteer Fire dept and Ellen and I went to see him march in the parade we then went back to the firehouse for a hotdog burger and beer

Later that day we went over to a friends for a house party

What did you do?

Take care continue on your book

Your friend
Jim

Janie Adams

Sheree Evans

From: Janie Adams
To: <Evasher6
Sent: Tuesday, July 30, 2013 1:27 PM
Subject: Fw: GM and Agent Orange

Subject: Re: GM and Agent Orange

Hi Sheree,

My name is Janie Adams. My husband was a Vietnam vet who died of GM. in 2006. I am seeking DIC. I'm searching for any research or any proof that I might use in my endeavor ie that links GM with Agent Orange in animals or simply links GM with Agent Orange, (any real evidence I can use).

Thank you in advance,
Janie Adams

Thank You Helpful Organizations

Life goes on

I want to give my heartfelt thanks to the organizations that helped me through my trying times. They are truly some of God's chosen angels on earth. These organizations have love, wisdom and the insight for helping those in trouble or in need. Each and every one of them strive daily to fight the Fight to Make it Right! The battles go on today. I pray their hours of devotion to the cause can help many others, as they did me.

Quilt of Tears:

http://www.agentorangequiltoftears.com/

They are called the
"Quilt of Tears"
for the many tears that have been shed by & for these victims.

About the squares of the Quilt of Tears written by Dale L. Ulmer...

Each square is sewn with loving hands
Carrying a message far across our land
Of soldiers battling an invisible rival
The war rages on in their fight for survival
Each soldiers name is sewn into the fabric of life
In memory of their courage, honor and strife
They are the hero's un-realized for their contribution
And are worthy of recognition and restitution
Therefore with each thread creating their name
Their sacrifice will not have been in vain
Remembrance of their struggle with Agent Oranges toll
Sewn in history is their story of unselfish hearts and brave souls

Fear not my great soldier...for your story shall be passed down throughout the years
Because the fabric of your life is sewn in the quilt of tears

Agent Orange Quilts of Tears

The Vietnam Veteran Agent Orange Quilts of Tears are a memorial, tribute and honor to our Agent Orange Victims, living and dead. who have suffered the after effects of the herbicides used in Vietnam. Herbicides were sprayed by aircraft to destroy foliage, thus denying the enemy ground cover and their food supply

Twenty million gallons of herbicides were used in Vietnam of which 12 million gallons was Agent Orange. Our service men were told it was harmless. We have found out since that the herbicides, including Agent Orange, causes may severe health problems and cancers. Agent Orange contained dioxin, the most toxic chemical developed by man

The quilt project was founded by Jennie Le Fevre, an Agent Orange widow, also President of the Agent Orange Victims and Widows Support Network, a non-profit organization.. The project was founded and established by Ms. Le Fevre, to honor and recoginize the plight of the Agent Orange Victims and their families. Agent Orange has been interwoven into fabric of lives of the victims and their families, the Quilts of Tears is their story, told eloquently by their own families in each block. The blocks are adorned with the victim's picture, their Vietnam service information, their health status as related to Agent Orange, etc, etc. The images sewn into the Quilts express the love, pain, and sorrow felt by the victims families. The blocks are then sewn into quilts that are displayed nationwide at Vietnam Veterans' reunions and functions.

Many health problems and cancers we believe to be a result of exposure to Agent Orange are not acknowledged by the Department of Veterans Affairs. Possibly 250,00 deaths had resulted from Agent and many families and widows have not been compensated for the loss of their loved ones. The veterans who are still living appreciate the honor and respect the Quilts of Tears give them. For the families who have lost someone to this great tragedy, the Quilts facilitate a healing process. It is said there is no room on the Vietnam Veterans Memorial Wall for these victims, but in our minds there is Room in our hearts and on these Quilts. Many have said they consider the Quilts of Tears as "The Other Side of the Wall." The Quilts of Tears are to draw a national attention of the Vietnam Veteran effected by the Agent Orange sprayed on them in Vietnam

The quilts are called the "Quilts of Tears" for many tears have been shed for these victims. One veteran stated that the "Quilts of Tears" was the most moving piece of art he had seen since the Wall in Washington, D.C. At present , there are 12 Quilts, each quilt contains 20 blocks, each quilt measures 80 x 100 inches. This Quilt project is one of a kind, dedicated solely to our Vietnam Agent Orange Victims only, at events, the Quilts of Tears are the only quilt display in America about Agent Orange.that solely represents the victims plight..

Wednesday, March 10, 2004 America Online: EvaSher6

Vietnam Veterans Wives:

http://www.vietnamveteranwives.org/

Vietnam Veteran Wives
helping all veterans and their families

Vietnam Veteran Wives, a 501(c)19 Non-Profit Veterans Service Organization, has been created to reach out to Veterans, their spouses and families. The time has come to take a stand. Vietnam Veteran Wives was created by the wife and widow of a Vietnam Veteran, who saw a much needed area for improvement, concerning subjects such as: Benefits for spouses and children, VA Claims, PTSD issues, DIC claims, informing veterans of what benefits are available to them and to their families, after their time in service. In addition to bringing to light the fact that the VA system leaves the Spouse and families of Veterans behind when it comes to services they provide.

Vietnam Veteran Wives is working hard to provide counselors for both individual and families, claims filing, making arrangements for transportation to local VAMC's, conducting "Stand-Downs" for veterans in rural areas to provide much needed clothing, blankets and socialization for Vets and their families. To provide a resource for Veterans and their spouse's to turn to for guidance as to the question "where do we go from here".

One of the main issues is the fact that during "out processing" most veterans do not obtain the knowledge of what is available to them. Vietnam Veteran Wives steps in here to be a solid backbone for the voices of Veterans and their families to turn to for that much needed knowledge and support.

Although the name is Vietnam Veteran Wives it is much more than that. Vietnam Veteran Wives is available to All Veterans and their Families. It doesn't matter if you were in during WWII, Korea, Vietnam, Lebanon, Granada, Beirut, Bosnia, Somalia, Persian Gulf, Operation Enduring Freedom or Operation Iraqi Freedom; Vietnam Veteran Wives is here for you.

Vietnam Veteran Wives works 100% with, and for all veterans throughout America. We network with women across America to determine the needs of our veterans and to establish the truth.

Danna Hughes

Monica Harvey

http://www.veteransmusicministry.com

Monica Harvey is a compelling singer using her talent to "Welcome Home" those Veterans lost and in need of a healed heart.

In 2001, Monica began traveling with Veteran Commanders through Nebraska to Veterans Homes, Hospitals, Psychiatric Wards and Correctional Centers. You can find her schedule on her website. Since 2004, she volunteers at Biker rallies, rides, Shows, Vietnam Vet reunions, National Memorials, Retreats, Tributes and traveling wall venues across the United States.

Aug. 25, 2001, during a Veterans parade, Monica was riding with the VFW State Commander in an antique wagon behind Percheron mares, something spooked the mares and in the resulting runaway they crashed into the back of a pickup. The driver broke his ribs, the State Commander severely broke his leg, another rider had to have shoulder surgery and suffered a bruised kidney. Monica flew 19 ft. through a "brown cloud" landing first on her right fist and jamming her right elbow and bruising her right leg. This extraordinary experience caught the attention of the Veteran Commanders and as a result they have adopted Monica as their "little sister".

We honor Gold Star Mothers, their families, Bikers with a Mission, and their contribution to the United States.

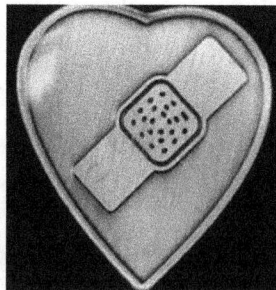

Donald Tate

Don Tate is a retired soldier and high school English teacher. Raised in a rural part of Brisbane, Australia, he went to the Vietnam War as a naive but patriotic infantryman and was badly wounded in action. After years of rehabilitation, he and his wife, Carole, have raised five children in the Shellharbour region of New South Wales, and in 2000, Don received the Australian Sports Medal for services to sport. He is an outspoken advocate for war veterans.

Don wrote an article that helped me get a lot of information about some of the things Tommy was experiencing. The article was titled The Guinea-Pigs of Vietnam and started out like this…

An examination of the effects of the chemicals and pesticides sprayed on the soldiers who fought in the Vietnam War. As well as my own research into the matter, I am indebted to my friend, Mrs. Jean Williams for her remarkable undertakings on this issue. © Don Tate

I'd like to invite you to get his book, The War Within.

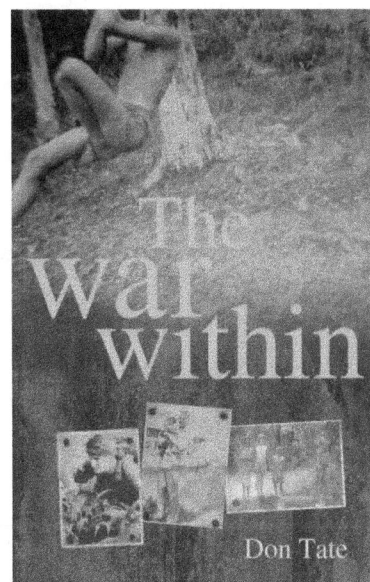

. . . a memoir that is at once dramatic, disturbing, sexually charged, and often very funny, but ultimately a moving portrait of a man who has found the inner strength to overcome . . . ' - Paul Ham, international journalist and author This is a complex, virtuoso analysis of an Australian life written by an unabashed and unrepentant author-an acidic dissection of the role that genes and environment have in developing a person's character, as well as a sauntering chronicle of social analysis. In turn, we follow the life of the author as he comes to terms with being a disaffected youth, a patriotic but naive infantryman in the Vietnam War, and an alienated, disabled veteran struggling with male status anxiety-apparently inexhaustible in its capacity to cause suffering. Along the way, Tate examines the dark crevices of the male psyche as he battles inner demons and the unconditional love of his beautiful Christian wife, Carole. Above all, this memoir is a celebration of the human condition and of a man with a can-do, cavalier attitude to life and his desire to rise above mediocrity. An outstanding contribution to Australia's rich heritage of memoir.

TIGER SHEREE

From:	"Donald Tate" <warvet_
To:	"TIGER SHEREE" <EVASHER6
Sent:	Wednesday, September 16, 2009 1:06 AM
Subject:	Re: Dapsone Tablets-Agent Orange

Well good luck to you Sheree. I trust you are successful in that claim. Bloody governments will use men, then discard them and their families when they're no longer of use. All the very, very best.

Don Tate
author, *"The War Within"* (Murdoch Books)
"...a raw and very powerful voice..." - **Bendigo Advertiser**

Debbie Sprague

www.detours2dreams.com

Debbie Sprague earned her bachelor's degree in therapeutic recreation, with a minor in psychology, graduating with honors from California State University (CSU), Chico. She also pursued postgraduate work in gerontology at CSU, Chico and University of Southern California (USC), Percy Andrus Gerontology Center. Her master's thesis, a successful grant proposal, brought the first Older America Act funds into Shasta County, California. The program she created has now been providing services to the community of Anderson, California for more than thirty years.

Debbie is also a board certified life/career coach and recreation therapist and holds a community college teaching credential in health and physical care services.

Debbie's life has been dedicated to improving the quality of life for others. She has worked with and/or created social service and health programs for the elderly and disabled, adaptive recreation programs for handicapped children, creative activities for residents in skilled nursing facilities, classes on independent living skills for seniors, and travel companies that specialize in providing escorted tours for senior citizens.

Debbie has personally experienced the challenges of caregiving during her son's losing battle with cancer and caring for her late mother-in-law. In 2004, Debbie's husband, a Vietnam veteran was diagnosed with complications from exposure to Agent Orange and Post-Traumatic Stress Disorder. Life dramatically changed for them, and in 2006, Debbie was also diagnosed with PTSD. Debbie then used her gift for creating programs to take on the challenge of finding answers and solutions for spouses who become overwhelmed and lost in the world of caregiving and PTSD.

Debbie is a grass-roots volunteer for Family of a Vet, where she is a contributing author for their web site and hosts the weekly blog radio show "Life after Combat – Caregiver Edition PTSD & TBI." She also provides workshops and community education on PTSD and secondary PTSD and is a contributor to the number one international bestseller *Wounded? Survive! Thrive!!!*

Debbie serves as the Vietnam veteran era representative on a focus committee for the National VA Caregiver Peer Support Mentoring Program. She is also an advisory group member for MOAA-Zieders "Warrior-Family Roundtable – Military Caregivers Financial-Legal Guide Advisory Group."

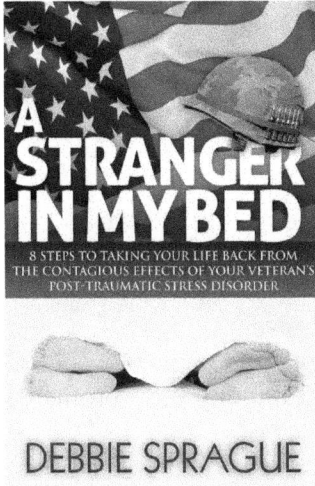

Combat-related PTSD and its effects on families that support wounded warriors is a growing concern throughout the world. This is a topic that few truly understand, and even fewer know how to help and support the veterans and families who are suffering. A Stranger in My Bed addresses these hidden topics and strives to provide empathy, compassion, education, and increased societal support for spouses and families who are facing the devastating effects of living with their veterans' PTSD. Tools and support are provided for those caring for our veterans to give them strength, hope, and wellness for their future. The unique five-part format uses story, education, and a self-help program to promote knowledge, compassion, and caregiver wellness. The story provides an intimate inside view of what PTSD looks like in a real-life family. The comprehensive, easy-to-read educational sections provide a wide range of topics on PTSD, including the effects on both the veteran and their families. The self-help program provides tools and skills to promote wellness and healing for caregivers and offers resources for ongoing support beyond the book.

Sheree Evans

From: "Debbie Sprague" <debbie
To: <evasher6
Sent: Wednesday, June 26, 2013 1:20 PM
Subject: Re: Widow wins Dic--Glio-Agent Orange-

Hi Sheree,

Thanks so much for getting in contact with me, and ordering my book. I would love to talk to you, the rest of my day is pretty hectic, I can give you a call this evening if that would be ok.

I look forward to talking with you.

A Brighter Tomorrow Begins Today,

Debbie Sprague, BCC, RT
Detours 2 Dreams ~ Specializing in Helping Spouse of Veterans With PTSD
www.detours2dreams.com

This is an organization Debbie supports by donating a portion of the author proceeds from A STRANGER IN MY BED.

www.familyofavet.com

Steven Andrade

Steven and I kind of adopted each other a couple of years ago. He's kind of like my little brother. I wanted to share this article from 417 Magazine about him. Such a special guy.

A Shattered Life, Reborn

Navy veteran **Steven Andrade** is working hard to overcome two decades of pain and suffering by helping younger vets do the same. **BY EVAN FISK**

A brown, fuzzy beard hugs his 46-year-old jaw as Steven Andrade reaches into his back pocket with his aching right hand. He pulls out a knife with a hand-forged steel blade, the handle carved from mastodon ivory. He made it himself, he says. Next thing you know, Steven is describing the supernatural parallels between God and this knife; the way the metal is purified and shaped, meticulously molded into a beautiful useful tool in the same way God works in a broken man's life. It's no surprise that Steven attended Central Bible College in Springfield. The sermonette is a rehearsed bit, though not insincere, and he repeats it nearly word for word days later, seeming to forget that he's told it before.

The blade folds and doubles over when Steven closes it, the same way his body did when he fell down a flight of metal stairs aboard the *U.S.S. St. Louis* 20 years ago. The etched ruts along the spine of the blade resemble the wrinkles on his otherwise-smooth cheeks, which scrunch up when he smiles.

You'll see that smile a lot if you spend any time with Steven. The smile isn't always a happy one, however. Behind those grinning teeth are two decades of pain, a domino trail of unfortunate events set into motion by a single false step. In 1986, Steven fell amid frantic activity aboard the *St. Louis*, mangling his strong body and changing his life forever. Steven has lived in constant pain since that day, but despite his troubles, Steven's still smiling, thanks largely to his involvement with a new foundation he's working with to help injured soldiers get the treatment they need.

A Sailor's Life Changes Forever

Steven's reason for joining the Navy is a simple one: "It was the only test I could pass," he says. He knew he wanted to serve in the armed forces somehow; he just needed the right opportunity. He attended CBC off and on for three years, studying sign language while there, though he never graduated because of nagging dyslexia and some strong disagreements with the school's Assemblies of God beliefs. At the time he attended CBC, he had hoped to work as a certified interpreter, but for reasons he can't remember, he ended up working for several local radio stations as a disc jockey. Then, in 1984, he enlisted in the Navy.

In the mid-1980s, Steven was stationed aboard the *U.S.S. St. Louis LKA-116*, a supply ship that sailed to various locations in the Pacific Ocean before being decommissioned in 1992. The quarters were tight, and although Steven doesn't consider himself a claustrophobic man, slipping into a bunk just inches from the mattress above you was enough to drive him crazy, especially since the crew was out to sea for three to four weeks at a time.

There is a picture of Steven in a golden frame that he still keeps to remind him of those days in the service. It's his boot camp picture (see opposite page). His cheeks are smooth and wrinkle-free. Look at him today, and it's hard to believe that it was only 20 years ago that the photo was taken. And although he doesn't quite look the same as he did at 23, Steven feels the patriotism that shines from his face in the photo to this very day. For example, he hates it when people talk bad about the president. "I don't agree with everything that past presidents have done, but they're still my commander-in-chief, and I have to respect the heck out of them," he says. He served his country and did it happily, he says. For more than a year in the Navy, he didn't have any problems. Then, in early 1986, everything changed in Steven's life.

The *St. Louis* was stationed in the waters off North Korea. Then the call came across the ship for General Quarters, or GQ, which is the phrase used to prepare a vessel for an incoming attack. (Think of a red alert on *Star Trek*.) Steven's ship was shooting 164-millimeter shells onto Russian soil at the time of the GQ, and word spread quickly that the North Koreans would soon be firing on the ship. In the rush to get to his correct post, Steven missed a step at the top of some metal stairs. The fall was bad. He hit every step as he fell down the flight of stairs, and when he finally reached the bottom, he was laying in an unnatural position, unable to stand.

This is where things got tricky. Here is Steven's version of the events: Because of the commotion of the drill, he wasn't immediately allowed to see the doctor. (When *417 Magazine* tried to confirm this, the Navy refused to comment other than stating that medical records are never open to the public.) In excruciating pain, Steven could barely walk for days after the GQ, once order was restored. It was two weeks before Steven was finally allowed to see the doctor. He blames the delay on his superior,

a man he worked with in the ship's kitchen Steven says the man had never liked him and didn't believe him when he claimed to be in extreme pain. It couldn't have helped that Steven had been to see the doctor on a regular basis before the accident, leading some to believe he was a hypochondriac. (Steven denies that he is one. "I just know when my body's in pain," he says.)

Finally, after seeing the doctor weeks later, he begged his superiors to allow him to have some X-rays done in Japan. His request fell

• Steven at age 46, 23 years after the picture on the opposite page was taken.

on deaf ears. For months Steven worked his normal post as a sus-chef, having to stand for most of the day to prepare meals for the crew. The pain was unbearable. The fall had shattered his tailbone and pinched several nerves in his back, yet he says he was never given pain medication. Finally he was allowed to get X-rays in Japan, and the results showed extensive damage. In addition to the shattered tailbone and pinched nerves, Steven also developed enuresis, a bed-wetting problem he attributes to a kidney infection. Soon after that, his request to leave the Navy was granted. One year, 11 months and 11 days after he joined the Navy, Steven was given a general discharge under honorable conditions. His time in the Navy was over, but the problems resulting from his experiences there were only beginning.

The Road to Recovery

Steven's physical troubles aren't a thing of the past. He mentions frequently that he's in terrible pain every day of his life. Time crawls when he wakes up in pain every morning, which makes each day stand out in his memory and drag on longer than it should.

Steven's physical ailments don't stop at a shattered tailbone. His fall in the Navy also left him with several pinched nerves in his back. He has degenerative arthritis, dyslexia, diabetes and carpal tunnel syndrome. His left leg is nearly an inch shorter than his right one, prompting him to wear custom shoes with an adjusted heel. He takes 20 different medications a day, several of them more than once a day. And although he says the military tried to argue that some of these problems existed before he entered the Navy, or were the result of hypochondria, he's had even more struggles that are too serious to ignore. His traumatic experiences led to two massive heart attacks before the age of 46, and as a result he now has four stents in his heart.

He also developed post-traumatic stress disorder. He can't pinpoint the exact cause of the PTSD—the fall, yes, and perhaps the time in San Miguel, in the Philippines, when guerilla snipers opened fire on Steven, missing his helmet by about an inch—but by the time he left the service, he was already seeing its effects. "I flipped... out on people," he says. Like yelling at them or becoming violent? He nods with an embarrassed smile, the same smile he flashes to keep the sadness at bay whenever it's time to recall painful memories. "I've learned to control myself," he continues. "I'm not a very emotional person. And when I do get emotional..." Steven never finishes the sentence. He just laughs and pokes at his Chinese food, which must be getting cold at the pace he's eating. A long, quiet 20 seconds go by before he picks up the conversation again. "After two major heart attacks, you can't really get upset," he says with a smile. "You just have to go with the flow."

Today, through years of therapy, he has mostly learned to curb any unannounced outbursts. Sure, there's the occasional loss of control, but he's still seeing a psychologist, which helps. Besides, at least in therapy, he has a way to actively overcome the disorder. The same can't be said for some of his other ailments. Even once Steven's back was X-rayed in Japan, he didn't receive any treatment for the excruciating pain until months after he returned home to Springfield, thinking the pain would decrease over time. Twenty years later, it still isn't gone.

After returning from the Navy, Steven struggled to qualify for disability. Because of

the bizarre circumstances of his accident, some of the records were missing from the Navy's files, leading to years of legal hassles in proving his ailments. As the legal struggles dragged on, Steve enrolled in Phillips Junior College—now Everest College, on West Sunshine Street in Springfield—to try to learn a trade so he could support himself until gaining disability. Having always been interested in medical work, especially after seeking out medical help of his own, he went to school to learn about medical office systems.

The will was there, but Steven's dyslexia got in the way, and, like college, he never finished his training. He looked for work, but no employers would hire him since his ailments made him uninsurable. He was still living at

• Making knives like these has become one of Steven's greatest passions in life.

home with his mother, and a feeling of deep depression and helplessness set in. Years later, he enrolled in classes as Vatterott College, once he was able to "get some help from Uncle Sam" in paying for the classes. He completed his courses, this time in commercial sign painting, and graduated in 1995. He painted every letter of each sign by hand, not using the vinyl lettering that most sign-makers use today. But his career was short-lived, as he soon developed carpal tunnel syndrome and had to abandon the trade he'd waited so long to learn. The carpal tunnel also rendered him useless in his original skill, sign language. He still knows the symbols, but he cannot always position his hands properly, and thus cannot be certified as a registered interpreter. It's like a painter going blind. It doesn't keep him from occasionally eavesdropping on a conversation between two deaf people, mind

you, and he hasn't lost all use of his hands. Those who don't know sign language would probably think the words and phrases he signs look fine. Steven tells with great pride of his sign language performance at a talent show aboard a cruise ship some years ago while vacationing with his mom. He stood in front of the large, crowded room of strangers and silently signed the Lord's Prayer. Tears filled the eyes of his fellow vacationers, he remembers, as those in attendance broke the perfect silence with thunderous applause and a standing ovation. But despite esteem-building performances such as this, Steven was still living at home with his mom, with whom he continues to live to this day near Pleasant Hope, north of Springfield. "Living at home with my mom... I'm not independent, basically," he says. "And I like my independence. [Living at home] makes me feel like I'm not complete."

In 20 years, Steven hasn't been able to keep many steady jobs. Sure, there was a gig as a security guard from time to time—even one for famed fallen televangelist Jimmy Swaggart—but never a career to call his own. Never anything to give Steven the sense of accomplishment he felt in his short service to the Navy. Nothing to make him feel complete. When asked about the one thing he's done in his life that he's most proud of, he shies away from the question, instead pointing out how helpful his mother and friends and even doctors have been.

In 2004, Steven was finally granted 100-percent disability coverage, 18 years after a mistake as simple as a bad step changed his life forever. With help from the D.A.V. and a signed affidavit from a fellow sailor, he was finally able to prove the severity of his injuries. With the government's recognition of his physical limitations came an end to his working days, even from part-time jobs. And though he jokes that he's retired now at the ripe old age of 46, he still has his hobbies. He has several handguns that he likes to shoot in the range inside Bass Pro Shops Outdoor World. He keeps a small .22-caliber pistol hidden in the door of his car; it's loaded when he pulls it out to show it off. There's also his .44 Magnum, the one he's most proud of. Whenever he talks about its 10-inch barrel, he holds his hands approximately two feet apart to show its length.

And there are his knives, of course. He's made 22 of them by hand, a hobby he learned from Ozark knife-maker Tom McGinnis. Steven visits Tom's workshop frequently

• Steven sits next to his mother, and other members of Our House Foundation.

throughout the week. It takes him about two days of work to complete one knife. It's a good hobby for Steven, because although he certainly has to use his hands, he can take his time to avoid aggravating his carpal tunnel syndrome. For the handles, he uses wood, mastodon ivory or even oosik, the Eskimo word for the penile bone of a walrus.

Our House

Steven still isn't a healed man. The pain he felt 10 years ago is the same pain he felt today getting out of bed. But while his scars remain—both physical and emotional—they've taken on a new meaning and given Steven a true calling for the first time in years. Today Steven is on the board of directors for the Our House Foundation, a nonprofit organization that soon hopes to give wounded soldiers returning from Iraq and Afghanistan a place to live and recuperate. The goal is to prevent them from being thrust back into society before they're ready.

The Our House foundation is the brainchild of Dr. Rita Spilken. A native of Brooklyn, New York, Spilken moved to Springfield in 1991 to attend Forest Institute of Professional Psychology. One day, while dining at a Shoney's restaurant in north Springfield, she slipped on an unmarked wet spot and hit her head, causing severe head trauma. Her hip also popped out of its joint, taking away much of her mobility. As she had her hip replaced and underwent neurological evaluations for her head, she became severely depressed and confused about life.

As she was searching for medical help for herself, Dr. Spilken met several soldiers returning from Iraq and Afghanistan who were injured, many of them struggling with PTSD. Empathizing with their pain because of her own physical struggles, she began to

think of ways that she could help. She stayed awake at night, thinking about what solutions there could be, until one night she woke up with a vision of a community where returning injured soldiers could live and interact with each other, with medical personnel on hand to help with the rehabilitation process.

In February of this year, Dr. Spilken met Janet Dooley, Steven's mother. When Janet heard of the idea for Our House, she volunteered to help however she could. Today, she works side by side with Dr. Spilken in

But while *his scars* remain—both physical and emotional—they've taken on a *new meaning* and given Steven a true calling for the first time in years.

organizing the foundation, with Steven and a few others lending their ideas and support along the way. Our House is currently still in the early stages of development as all of the legal details get worked out and funds are raised, but the program is already organizing a guest speaker series, bringing in experts from various medical fields to speak on ways that soldiers can take steps toward returning to normal life.

The ultimate goal of The Our House Foundation is the creation of the "Welcome Homes." Spilken and Dooley are currently in negotiations to secure a building near Springfield as a site for the rehabilitation community. They hope that the building will not only house state-of-the-art medical equipment, but also provide shelter for dozens of soldiers from the current war who return

home with serious injuries or PTSD. Soldiers will rehabilitate and receive medical attention on site, surrounded by others with similar ailments who can relate to their problems. The foundation also hopes to have a store on location at the Welcome Homes center, so the veterans can practice simple tasks like counting change and interacting with customers before being thrust into work environments. And while there is no deadline for these facilities to be in place as of press time, the foundation has been moving forward quickly in its first year.

As for Steven, Our House has given him that purpose he's been missing for years. It's exactly the type of environment he wishes he'd had when returning home from the Navy, even though he wasn't technically serving during a time of war. And although he's had to trudge through life without the help of organizations like Our House, he's eager to share his experiences with others in hopes of helping them capitalize on opportunities he never had.

He smiles now, all the time in fact. Some of the time he's smiling as a defense mechanism, like when he grins in the middle of harsh stories about his years of depression. (Humor takes the place of that pain, he says.) But more and more, he's smiling because he's got a reason to wake up in the morning and a reason to leave the house and interact with people again. Our House has already affected the life of this sailor, and he's going to do everything he can to see that the foundation will do the same for many others like him.

By the Grace of God a Promise Kept

When we met we fell in love,
two blessings from God up above.
We dated, wed, started our life,
I was so happy to be his wife.
Two lonely hearts became one,
caring & sharing we started our fun.
The more I learned about his life,
I realized his pain and strife.
The boy who went to war in Vietnam,
came back home a broken man,
but the public didn't give a damn.
As the years went by, Agent Orange took his health, too,
VA in denial, many veterans didn't know what to do.
He loved his country and comrades in war,
too soon he met those brothers at Heaven's door.
His life cut short from cancer in his brain,
Glioblastoma was its name.
I swear his death will not be in vain.
The promise I gave in his final days,
the one thing he wanted...the government to pay.
I started the fight to make it right.
It took me eight years and money was tight.
I hired lawyers, Bergmann & Moore.
Many denials & appeals were in store.
Then the phone rang, on that fateful day,
I won my case, the government would pay.
By the grace of God a promise kept.
In my heart I'll never forget.
Your true love is all I need.
Tommy, in my heart you'll always be

Tiger,
Sheree

Note from the Author

I'd like to say thank you for purchasing my book. It means a lot to me to be able to share my journey through the good and bad times.

Thanks to God Almighty for giving me the strength to stand for what I knew was right. He helped me grow and I hope to pass my strength and knowledge to other widows and Vietnam Vets who suffer from Glio. I hope in some way this book will help you win in seeking your benefits.

Tommy was loaned to me by our Lord and Savior for a short time. I was truly blessed to be touched with a love that will last forever. I look forward to seeing my Tommy again in Heaven.

Over the last couple of years I have suffered from some sever health issues. Thankfully I am well on my way to recovery. Again, God has been good to me.

Tommy's dream and my goal…pay it forward. This is a big reason I wrote this book. With the help of many friends and acquaintances, I feel those dreams are coming true. I have already started a sequel and look forward to sharing more stories with you.

Please remember it's better in numbers then by one. You can contact me, at evasher6@cebridge.net.

God Bless!

Tiger Sheree

References

Operation Red dragonfly. Check out Facebook page
https://www.facebook.com/operationreddragonfly1

Agent Orange Zone
http://agentorangezone.blogspot.com/2011/02/va-links-brain-cancer-to-agentorange.html

Cold war veterans blog
http://cold-war-veterans-blog.blogspot.com

prweb
http://news.yahoo.com/s/prweb/20110217/bs_prweb/prweb5080394.htm

Daily Health Reviews
http://www.hanliumm1.com/latest-cancer-news-35

One Old Vet
http://oneoldvet.com/?p=26352

Veterans Today
http://www.veteranstoday.com/2011/02/17/never-ever-give-up-on-veterans-claims
http://www.prweb.com/releases/2011/02/prweb5080394.htm

Lawyers and Settlements. com
http://www.lawyersandsettlements.com/articles/va-disability-benefits/va-benefits-disability

Here are several references that were helpful to me when I was working on my DIC widow's case.

http://www.veteranstoday.com/2011/02/17/never-ever-give-up-on-veterans-claims/

http://www.geocities.com/pentagon/bunker/8212/briefc3.html?200724

http://www.cancer.org/docroot/PED/content/PED_1_3x_agent_orange_and_cancer.asp

http://aolsvc.health.webmd.aol.com/content/article/6/1680_53558.htm?SRC=aolkw=encephalitis

http://sarge5575.com/agentorange.html

http://www.american.edu/TED/ice/vietnam.htm

http://aolsvc.health.webmd.aol.com/content/healthwise/258/87068.htm

http://www.emedicine.com/med/topic138.htm

http://vva.org/Agent Orange/index.htm

http://tcrc.acor.org./staging.html

http://www.onlinelawyerssourse.com/dioxin/vietnam.html

http://aje.oxfordjournals.org/content/129/6/1187.abstract

http://www.sfgate.com/health/article/SF-VA-brain-research-technology-advance-3751773

http://www.healthatoz.com/healthatoz/Atoz/ency/choriocarcinoma.jsp

http://www.biausa.org/Pages/causes_of_brain_injury.html

http://subtlebraininjury.com/vestibular1.html

http://www.jsonline.com/business/researchers-awarded-grant-to-study-brain-tumor-therapie

http://www.veteranstoday.com/2010/07/18/va-sec-shinseki-and-agent-orange-advocates-get-win

http://www.members.tripod.com/warvet_69/guineapig.htm

http://cybersarges.tripod.com/johnstoniland.html

http://www.usvetdsp.com/agentorange.htm

http://www.silverrose.info/qualifying%20diseases.html

http://www.silverrose.info/quilt%20of%20tears.html

http://pub44.bravenet.com/guestbook/370774980

http://tabbykatus.tripod.com/myquiethero/id6.html

http://www.va.gov/vetapp/files1/9404982.txt

http://randomlyrandomrick.blogspot.com/2007/04/memorial-day-ramblings.html

http://www.2ndbattalion94thartillery.com/Chas/HouseCom.htm

http://malcontends.blogspot.com/2007/05/vet-imprisoned-for-seeking-benefits_02.html

http://agentorangezone.blogspot.com/2011/07/widow-of-veteran-granted-benefits-after.html

http://www.hotkey.net.au/~marshalle/dapsonel/dapsonel.htm

http://www.geocities.com/Pentagon/Bunker/8212/dioxinkills.html?200724

http://aowac.org/aboutao/index.html

http://homestead.com/quilt_of_tears/files/story.htm

http://www.nationsencyclopedia.com/Asia-and-Oceania/Vietnam-HEALTH.html

http://www.ibiblio.org/pub/academic/history/marshall/military/vietnam/nvet_archive/nveto

http://www.tpromo.com/usvi/agent-d5.htm

http://aolsvc.health.webmd.aol.com/content/article/8/1680_54131.htm

http://www.madsci.org/posts/archives/jun99/928942463.me.r.html
http://www.1stmarinedivisionassociation.org/operation-battles-folder/operation_ranch_hand

http://www.wapd.org/points/dcorbin/nv/TCDDinfo/default.htm

http://www.deltronix.com/public/li/lymph.html

http://www.zoomph.net/diabetes.world/gastroparesis.htm

http://www.lungusa.org/diseases/ards_factsheet.html

http://www.emedicine.com/ent/topic306.htm

We have many organizations caring for their fellow comrades—and understand the demand for much needed help, the following is just a few contacts, friends, brothers, and sisters. Acknowledgements—Veterans helping Veterans!

VA web on AO—
http://www.vba.va.gov/bln/21/benefits/Herbicide/AOno3.htm

Veterans for Change—
Veterans-For-Change, Inc
Founder and CEO—Jim Davis

Home Front Vet. Org—
Veterans For Peace/ American Legion post #140

Marine Veteran, Brother Aaron Davis

Hope Farms for Veterans—PTSD Awareness
Founder—Unknown Vet, Brother Bob Mimes

Veterans Music Ministry.com

Founder—Monica Harvey—husband Bob

Veterans Recreation & Rehabilitation Center—
Vetrecrehabcenter.org
President & CEO Brother Charles Rennaker

On Target for Veterans—
http://www.ontarget4veterans.org
President & CEO Brother Roger Werner

Vital Eco Solutions Inc.
http://www.vitalecosolutions.com
President & CEO—Todd Keyes

Hope 4 PTSD Vets—
http://www.hope4ptsdvets.org
Director—Melissa/ Exec—Kevin Taylor

Family of a Vet—
Familyofavet.com

Lynn Morris—Missouri House of Representatives and Owner of Family Pharmacy

Cruisin' USA, Event plan June, 2014 in Nixa, MO—Director of Business—Brian Bingham

Our House Foundation—
Ourhousefoundation.org
Founder—Dr. Rita Spilken, PTSD and TBIs Vets from Iraq and Afghanistan

Hopefully, VFW #3404 Springfield, MO. And American Legion—St. Louis, MO and or Springfield, MO

Upcoming acknowledgements—Springfield Writer's Guild, Springfield, MO
www.missouriwritersguild.org
President Yvonne Erwin

And especially to my friend, auxiliary publisher, Sharon Kizziah-Holmes
Owner New auxiliary publishing company—Paperback Press

About the publisher

Paperback-Press

Visions, imaginings, dreams….everyone in every walk of life has them; for writers, being published is one of those dreams. However, the reality of it is that most writers aren't accepted up by a traditional publisher. Does that stop you from still wanting to follow that dream? Not at all! *Paperback-Press* is here to help you make your dream come true.

Paperback-Press was founded by independent author Sharon Kizziah-Holmes and her husband Dennis. Sharon has been assisting writers in self-publishing since the mid 1990's. Recently she observed many colleagues were under-compensated and under-served by small press/hybrid publishers (who typically require certain rights, demand purchase of a designated number of books and receive a portion of the author's royalties). As a result of this discovery, she developed *PBP*, an affordable, professional indie assist publishing venue.

As a value-added, indie assist service provider, *Paperback-Press* works for independent authors who may utilize *PBP's* publishing brand, while retaining the rights of a self-published author. (However, there is no obligation to use their brands or logos.) *Paperback-Press* does *not* require a minim amount book purchase, does *not* receive royalties and the author keeps *%100* of his or her rights.

PBP has also published for a number of well-established authors who previously had arrangements with traditional publishers. These authors see the value in partnering with this new company to re-release their titles. One such client is romance author Lori Copeland.

Now, more than ever, independent authors have a plethora of opportunities available to get their stories to the readers, and *PBP* hopes to be your choice. Your Writing + Our Expertise = Success is our motto. As your publishing partner, we will help you produce a product you can be proud of, market and sell.

In essence, *PBP* offers a unique option between the author doing all the work themselves before self-publishing, and an author being accepted and published by a traditional house. If you are ready to publish your novel, short story/stories, memoir, novella, picture book…*Paperback-Press* is the indie assist publisher for you!

What are some benefits Paperback-Press offers?

- **PBP** accepts electronic submissions only (unless otherwise agreed upon by both parties)
- An official proposal for the project is sent to the author
- Upon acceptance of proposal, a service agreement is offered that protects the author and the service provider
- The author is involved with the projects creation process - from cover design to the finished product
- Cover design, illustrators for children's books and assignment of ISBNs are included
- e-book formatting and publishing. (Kindle and NOOK)
- Paperback formatting and publishing is expertly completed, with expanded distribution channels through the CreateSpace print on demand service
- Picture book formatting for print and e-book are included
- **PBP** takes no royalties. 100% of all royalties from paperback or digital sales remain with the author
- All rights remain with the author. i.e.: authorship, ownership, copyright, printing rights etc.
- Upon completion, a PDF proof of the publication will be sent to the author for approval
- **PBP** ensures that work complies with industry standards, and quality, prior to publishing
- **PBP** commits that the project will be published within six months of the execution of the agreement
- An author page is developed and included on the **Paperback-Press** website when the PBP brand/logo is used
- Independent publishing is available for authors who want to self-publish using only PBP's expertise
- Paperback-Press, Kids Book Press Publishing, e-book Press Publishing & Audio Book Press are all imprints of A & S Publishing, A & S Holmes, Inc.

Sharon Kizziah-Holmes – Publishing Coordinator

These are things other soldiers wrote on the back cover of Tommy's Vietnam 'Short Timer Calendar' just before Tommy got to come home.